TEACHER'S PET PUBLICATIONS

PUZZLE PACK
for
E. A. Poe Stories
based on the stories and poems by
Edgar Allan Poe

Written by
William T. Collins

© 2005 Teacher's Pet Publications
All Rights Reserved

The materials in this packet are copyrighted
by Teacher's Pet Publications, Inc.

These pages may be duplicated by the purchaser
for use in the purchaser's own classroom.

Copying any of these materials and distributing them
for any other purpose is a violation of the copyright laws.

© 2005 Teacher's Pet Publications, Inc.
www.tpet.com

INTRODUCTION
If you already own the LitPlan for this title, this Puzzle Pack will refresh your Unit Resource Materials and Vocabulary Resource Materials sections plus give you additional materials you can substitute into the tests. If you do not already have a complete LitPlan, these pages will give you some supplemental materials to use with your own plan. There are two main groups of materials: one set for unit words (such as characters' names, symbols, places, etc.) and one set for vocabulary words associated with the book.

WORD LIST
There is a word list for both the unit words and the vocabulary words. These lists show you which words are being used in the materials and the clues or definitions being used for those words. You may want to give students a word list with clues/definitions to help them, or you may want students to only have a word list (without clues/definitions) if you want them to work a little harder. Both are available for duplication. The word lists can also be your "calling key" for the bingo games.

FILL IN THE BLANK AND MATCHING
There are 4 each of the fill in the blank and matching worksheets for both the unit and vocabulary words. These pages can be used either as extra worksheets for students or as objective parts of a unit test. They can be done individually if students need extra help or as a whole class activity to review the material covered.

MAGIC SQUARES
The magic squares not only reinforce the material covered but also work on reasoning and math skills. Many teachers have told us that their students really enjoy doing these!

WORD SEARCH PUZZLES
The word search words go in all directions, as indicated on your answer keys. Two of the word search puzzles have the clues listed rather than the words. This makes the puzzle a little more difficult, but it reinforces the material better. Two word search puzzles have words only for students who find the clue puzzles too difficult.

CROSSWORD PUZZLES
Both unit and vocabulary word sections have 4 crossword puzzles.

BINGO CARDS
There are 32 individual bingo cards for the unit words and 32 individual bingo cards for the vocabulary words. You can use your word list as a "call list," calling the words at random and marking them off of your list as you go, or you could use the flash cards by cutting them apart and drawing the words at random from a hat (or box or whatever). To make a better review, you might ask for the definition and spelling of each word as you call it out–or you could call out the definitions and have students tell you the words they need to look for on the puzzle.

JUGGLE LETTERS
The vocabulary juggle letter game is intended to help students learn the spellings of the words. One sheet has the definitions listed on it as an extra help for students who need it or to reinforce the definitions if you choose to do so.

FLASH CARDS
We've included a set of vocabulary flash cards you can duplicate, cut, and fold for your students. Some teachers make a few sets for general use by the class; others make a set for each student. Some teachers duplicate them for each student and have the students cut & fold their own. You can cut out just the words and put them in a hat, have each student pick out one word and write the definition and a sentence for that word. Students then swap words and papers, with the next student adding a sentence of his own under the last one. You can have students swap as many times as you like. Each time the student will read the sentences written prior to his own and then add a sentence. You can cut out the words and definitions separately and play "I Have; Who Has?" Each student in the room draws a word and definition. The first student says, "I have (the name of the word). Who has the definition?" The student with the definition reads it then says, "I have (the name of the vocabulary word she has). Who has the definition?" The round continues until all words and definitions have been given.

Poe Stories Word List

No.	Word	Clue/Definition
1.	AMONTILLADO	Cask of _____ (CA)
2.	ANNABEL	_____ Lee; she lived in a kingdom by the sea
3.	AXE	Narrator murdered his wife with one (BC)
4.	BELLS	To the rhyming and chiming of the _____
5.	BOOK	Narrator met Dupin looking for the same rare _____ (RM)
6.	CASK	_____ of Amontillado (CA)
7.	CAT	The Black _____ (BC)
8.	CHAIR	Murderer placed his _____ over the place where he put the corpse
9.	CHIMNEY	Place narrator disposed of his wife's body (BC)
10.	COSTUMES	What people wore to the ball (MRD)
11.	DEATH	Red _____; a highly contagious disease (MRD)
12.	DETECTIVE	Dupin was the _____ (RM)
13.	DUNGEON	Setting for the story (PP)
14.	DUPIN	The detective (RM)
15.	EBONY	Color of clock (MRD)
16.	ESPANAYE	Madame L'_____ and Mademoiselle Camille L' _____ (RM)
17.	EYE	Vulture___ (TTH)
18.	FACSIMILE	Dupin replaced the letter with a _____ (PL)
19.	FLOOR	The murderer put the corpse under the _____ boards (TTH)
20.	FOOD	Narrator put this on the ropes (PP)
21.	GALLOWS	Narrator thought white on the second cat's breast looked like_____
22.	GOTHIC	Kind of story with mansion, dark tombs beneath/inside; ominous setting, living corpse (FHU)
23.	HEART	The Tell-Tale _____ (TTH)
24.	HOUSE	Narrator's _____ burned down, leaving figure of a cat and rope on one wall (BC)
25.	LEBON	Person accused of murders in Rue St. Morgue (RM)
26.	LETTER	It was stolen (PL)
27.	LUCHESI	Montresor said he could taste the wine if Fortunato were busy
28.	MAD	Crazy (TTH)
29.	MADELINE	Lady _____ (FHU)
30.	MASQUE	_____ of Red Death (MRD)
31.	MONTRESOR	He decided to kill Fortunato (CA)
32.	MUTILATED	Condition of Madame L'Espanaye's corpse (RM)
33.	NEVERMORE	Quoth the Raven '_____'
34.	PENDULUM	The Pit and The _____ (PP)
35.	PIT	The _____ and The Pendulum (PP)
36.	PLUTO	The cat's name (BC)
37.	POLICE	Murderer greeted them warmly (TTH)
38.	PROPSPERO	The Prince (MRD)
39.	PURLOINED	The _____ Letter (PL)
40.	RATS	Narrator wanted them to eat the ropes (PP)
41.	RAVEN	Quoth the _____ 'Nevermore'
42.	RECESS	Montresor bricked Fortunato into a _____ in the wall (CA)
43.	RED	Masque of _____ Death (MRD)
44.	REVENGE	Montresor's motive (CA)
45.	RODERICK	Mr. Usher (FHU)
46.	ROPE	Narrator hanged his cat with one (BC)
47.	SAILOR	The ourang-outang belonged to him (RM)
48.	SEVEN	Number of rooms in use at the Prince's ball (MRD)
49.	SUFFOCATED	How the old man died (TTH)

Poe Stories Word List

No.	Word	Clue/Definition
50.	TROWEL	Sign of a mason (CA)
51.	TWIN	Usher put his ____ sister's body in a vault (FHU)
52.	USHER	Fall of the House of ____ (FHU)
53.	VAULT	Place where Usher put his twin sister's body (FHU)
54.	WALLS	They moved inward (PP)

Poe Stories Fill In The Blanks 1

1. The Prince (MRD)
2. Setting for the story (PP)
3. Montresor's motive (CA)
4. Narrator hanged his cat with one (BC)
5. Narrator's ____ burned down, leaving figure of a cat and rope on one wall (BC)
6. Narrator murdered his wife with one (BC)
7. Narrator wanted them to eat the ropes (PP)
8. Narrator met Dupin looking for the same rare____ (RM)
9. Vulture____(TTH)
10. The ____ and The Pendulum (PP)
11. The ourang-outang belonged to him (RM)
12. How the old man died (TTH)
13. Crazy (TTH)
14. Number of rooms in use at the Prince's ball (MRD)
15. ____Lee; she lived in a kingdom by the sea
16. Quoth the ____ 'Nevermore'
17. Narrator thought white on the second cat's breast looked like____
18. Dupin replaced the letter with a ____(PL)
19. Madame L'____ and Mademoiselle Camille L'____ (RM)
20. Condition of Madame L'Espanaye's corpse (RM)

Poe Stories Fill In The Blanks 1 Answer Key

PROPSPERO	1. The Prince (MRD)
DUNGEON	2. Setting for the story (PP)
REVENGE	3. Montresor's motive (CA)
ROPE	4. Narrator hanged his cat with one (BC)
HOUSE	5. Narrator's ____ burned down, leaving figure of a cat and rope on one wall (BC)
AXE	6. Narrator murdered his wife with one (BC)
RATS	7. Narrator wanted them to eat the ropes (PP)
BOOK	8. Narrator met Dupin looking for the same rare____ (RM)
EYE	9. Vulture____(TTH)
PIT	10. The ____ and The Pendulum (PP)
SAILOR	11. The ourang-outang belonged to him (RM)
SUFFOCATED	12. How the old man died (TTH)
MAD	13. Crazy (TTH)
SEVEN	14. Number of rooms in use at the Prince's ball (MRD)
ANNABEL	15. ____Lee; she lived in a kingdom by the sea
RAVEN	16. Quoth the ____ 'Nevermore'
GALLOWS	17. Narrator thought white on the second cat's breast looked like____
FACSIMILE	18. Dupin replaced the letter with a ____(PL)
ESPANAYE	19. Madame L'____ and Mademoiselle Camille L'____ (RM)
MUTILATED	20. Condition of Madame L'Espanaye's corpse (RM)

Poe Stories Fill In The Blanks 2

_____

1. Narrator hanged his cat with one (BC)
2. The cat's name (BC)
3. ____ of Red Death (MRD)
4. Murderer greeted them warmly (TTH)
5. Montresor said he could taste the wine if Fortunato were busy
6. Narrator thought white on the second cat's breast looked like____
7. The murderer put the corpse under the ____ boards(TTH)
8. Usher put his ____ sister's body in a vault (FHU)
9. ____Lee; she lived in a kingdom by the sea
10. The Prince (MRD)
11. Montresor bricked Fortunato into a ____ in the wall (CA)
12. How the old man died (TTH)
13. Crazy (TTH)
14. Cask of _____(CA)
15. To the rhyming and chiming of the ____
16. Fall of the House of ____ (FHU)
17. Quoth the Raven '____'
18. The detective (RM)
19. Condition of Madame L'Espanaye's corpse (RM)
20. ____ of Amontillado (CA)

Poe Stories Fill In The Blanks 2 Answer Key

ROPE	1. Narrator hanged his cat with one (BC)
PLUTO	2. The cat's name (BC)
MASQUE	3. ____ of Red Death (MRD)
POLICE	4. Murderer greeted them warmly (TTH)
LUCHESI	5. Montresor said he could taste the wine if Fortunato were busy
GALLOWS	6. Narrator thought white on the second cat's breast looked like____
FLOOR	7. The murderer put the corpse under the ____ boards(TTH)
TWIN	8. Usher put his ____ sister's body in a vault (FHU)
ANNABEL	9. ____Lee; she lived in a kingdom by the sea
PROPSPERO	10. The Prince (MRD)
RECESS	11. Montresor bricked Fortunato into a ____ in the wall (CA)
SUFFOCATED	12. How the old man died (TTH)
MAD	13. Crazy (TTH)
AMONTILLADO	14. Cask of ____(CA)
BELLS	15. To the rhyming and chiming of the ____
USHER	16. Fall of the House of ____ (FHU)
NEVERMORE	17. Quoth the Raven '____'
DUPIN	18. The detective (RM)
MUTILATED	19. Condition of Madame L'Espanaye's corpse (RM)
CASK	20. ____ of Amontillado (CA)

Poe Stories Fill In The Blanks 3

1. The Tell-Tale ____ (TTH)
2. It was stolen (PL)
3. Place narrator disposed of his wife's body (BC)
4. Narrator thought white on the second cat's breast looked like____
5. ____ of Red Death (MRD)
6. The detective (RM)
7. The ____ Letter (PL)
8. Crazy (TTH)
9. Narrator's ____ burned down, leaving figure of a cat and rope on one wall (BC)
10. Cask of _____ (CA)
11. They moved inward (PP)
12. Sign of a mason (CA)
13. The Black ____ (BC)
14. Setting for the story (PP)
15. Murderer placed his ____ over the place where he put the corpse
16. ____ Lee; she lived in a kingdom by the sea
17. Narrator murdered his wife with one (BC)
18. He decided to kill Fortunato (CA)
19. Quoth the ____ 'Nevermore'
20. Dupin was the ____ (RM)

Poe Stories Fill In The Blanks 3 Answer Key

HEART	1. The Tell-Tale ____ (TTH)
LETTER	2. It was stolen (PL)
CHIMNEY	3. Place narrator disposed of his wife's body (BC)
GALLOWS	4. Narrator thought white on the second cat's breast looked like____
MASQUE	5. ____ of Red Death (MRD)
DUPIN	6. The detective (RM)
PURLOINED	7. The ____ Letter (PL)
MAD	8. Crazy (TTH)
HOUSE	9. Narrator's ____ burned down, leaving figure of a cat and rope on one wall (BC)
AMONTILLADO	10. Cask of ____ (CA)
WALLS	11. They moved inward (PP)
TROWEL	12. Sign of a mason (CA)
CAT	13. The Black ____ (BC)
DUNGEON	14. Setting for the story (PP)
CHAIR	15. Murderer placed his ____ over the place where he put the corpse
ANNABEL	16. ____ Lee; she lived in a kingdom by the sea
AXE	17. Narrator murdered his wife with one (BC)
MONTRESOR	18. He decided to kill Fortunato (CA)
RAVEN	19. Quoth the ____ 'Nevermore'
DETECTIVE	20. Dupin was the ____ (RM)

Poe Stories Fill In The Blanks 4

_____

_____

_____

_____

_____

_____

_____

_____

_____

_____

_____

_____

_____

_____

_____

_____

_____

_____

_____

_____

1. Fall of the House of ____ (FHU)
2. Quoth the Raven '____'
3. Cask of ____ (CA)
4. Crazy (TTH)
5. They moved inward (PP)
6. The detective (RM)
7. Montresor's motive (CA)
8. Color of clock (MRD)
9. Red ____; a highly contagious disease (MRD)
10. The murderer put the corpse under the ____ boards(TTH)
11. Setting for the story (PP)
12. Usher put his ____ sister's body in a vault (FHU)
13. Dupin replaced the letter with a ____ (PL)
14. Masque of ____ Death (MRD)
15. Sign of a mason (CA)
16. Narrator thought white on the second cat's breast looked like____
17. ____ of Red Death (MRD)
18. The cat's name (BC)
19. What people wore to the ball (MRD)
20. The ____ Letter (PL)

Poe Stories Fill In The Blanks 4 Answer Key

USHER	1. Fall of the House of ____ (FHU)
NEVERMORE	2. Quoth the Raven '____'
AMONTILLADO	3. Cask of ____ (CA)
MAD	4. Crazy (TTH)
WALLS	5. They moved inward (PP)
DUPIN	6. The detective (RM)
REVENGE	7. Montresor's motive (CA)
EBONY	8. Color of clock (MRD)
DEATH	9. Red ____; a highly contagious disease (MRD)
FLOOR	10. The murderer put the corpse under the ____ boards (TTH)
DUNGEON	11. Setting for the story (PP)
TWIN	12. Usher put his ____ sister's body in a vault (FHU)
FACSIMILE	13. Dupin replaced the letter with a ____ (PL)
RED	14. Masque of ____ Death (MRD)
TROWEL	15. Sign of a mason (CA)
GALLOWS	16. Narrator thought white on the second cat's breast looked like ____
MASQUE	17. ____ of Red Death (MRD)
PLUTO	18. The cat's name (BC)
COSTUMES	19. What people wore to the ball (MRD)
PURLOINED	20. The ____ Letter (PL)

Poe Stories Matching 1

___ 1. DUPIN   A. Lady ____ (FHU)
___ 2. BOOK   B. The murderer put the corpse under the ____ boards(TTH)
___ 3. RAVEN   C. He decided to kill Fortunato (CA)
___ 4. RATS   D. Color of clock (MRD)
___ 5. CAT   E. Masque of ____ Death (MRD)
___ 6. SAILOR   F. The Prince (MRD)
___ 7. ROPE   G. Montresor's motive (CA)
___ 8. MONTRESOR   H. Crazy (TTH)
___ 9. FOOD   I. ____ of Amontillado (CA)
___10. MAD   J. The detective (RM)
___11. AMONTILLADO   K. Narrator thought white on the second cat's breast looked like____
___12. GALLOWS   L. The ourang-outang belonged to him (RM)
___13. RODERICK   M. It was stolen (PL)
___14. EBONY   N. Narrator met Dupin looking for the same rare____ (RM)
___15. LETTER   O. They moved inward (PP)
___16. PROPSPERO   P. Quoth the ____ 'Nevermore'
___17. FLOOR   Q. Narrator wanted them to eat the ropes (PP)
___18. WALLS   R. Cask of ____(CA)
___19. REVENGE   S. Vulture___(TTH)
___20. CHIMNEY   T. Madame L'____ and Mademoiselle Camille L'____ (RM)
___21. MADELINE   U. The Black ____ (BC)
___22. ESPANAYE   V. Mr. Usher (FHU)
___23. EYE   W. Narrator put this on the ropes (PP)
___24. CASK   X. Narrator hanged his cat with one (BC)
___25. RED   Y. Place narrator disposed of his wife's body (BC)

Poe Stories Matching 1 Answer Key

J - 1. DUPIN
N - 2. BOOK
P - 3. RAVEN
Q - 4. RATS
U - 5. CAT
L - 6. SAILOR
X - 7. ROPE
C - 8. MONTRESOR
W - 9. FOOD
H - 10. MAD
R - 11. AMONTILLADO
K - 12. GALLOWS
V - 13. RODERICK
D - 14. EBONY
M - 15. LETTER
F - 16. PROPSPERO
B - 17. FLOOR
O - 18. WALLS
G - 19. REVENGE
Y - 20. CHIMNEY
A - 21. MADELINE
T - 22. ESPANAYE
S - 23. EYE
I - 24. CASK
E - 25. RED

A. Lady _____ (FHU)
B. The murderer put the corpse under the _____ boards (TTH)
C. He decided to kill Fortunato (CA)
D. Color of clock (MRD)
E. Masque of _____ Death (MRD)
F. The Prince (MRD)
G. Montresor's motive (CA)
H. Crazy (TTH)
I. _____ of Amontillado (CA)
J. The detective (RM)
K. Narrator thought white on the second cat's breast looked like_____
L. The ourang-outang belonged to him (RM)
M. It was stolen (PL)
N. Narrator met Dupin looking for the same rare_____ (RM)
O. They moved inward (PP)
P. Quoth the _____ 'Nevermore'
Q. Narrator wanted them to eat the ropes (PP)
R. Cask of _____ (CA)
S. Vulture___(TTH)
T. Madame L'_____ and Mademoiselle Camille L' _____ (RM)
U. The Black _____ (BC)
V. Mr. Usher (FHU)
W. Narrator put this on the ropes (PP)
X. Narrator hanged his cat with one (BC)
Y. Place narrator disposed of his wife's body (BC)

Poe Stories Matching 2

___ 1. BELLS   A. To the rhyming and chiming of the ____
___ 2. LETTER   B. Masque of ____ Death (MRD)
___ 3. VAULT   C. Condition of Madame L'Espanaye's corpse (RM)
___ 4. GALLOWS   D. Narrator thought white on the second cat's breast looked like____
___ 5. EBONY   E. Montresor said he could taste the wine if Fortunato were busy
___ 6. FACSIMILE   F. The cat's name (BC)
___ 7. RODERICK   G. Mr. Usher (FHU)
___ 8. MAD   H. It was stolen (PL)
___ 9. DUPIN   I. Dupin replaced the letter with a ____(PL)
___10. COSTUMES   J. Murderer greeted them warmly (TTH)
___11. GOTHIC   K. What people wore to the ball (MRD)
___12. MUTILATED   L. How the old man died (TTH)
___13. PLUTO   M. Dupin was the ____ (RM)
___14. ANNABEL   N. Color of clock (MRD)
___15. FOOD   O. The detective (RM)
___16. DETECTIVE   P. Crazy (TTH)
___17. WALLS   Q. Quoth the Raven '____'
___18. SUFFOCATED   R. Kind of story with mansion, dark tombs beneath/inside; ominous setting, living corpse (FHU)
___19. NEVERMORE   S. They moved inward (PP)
___20. POLICE   T. Narrator put this on the ropes (PP)
___21. RED   U. Fall of the House of ____ (FHU)
___22. LUCHESI   V. The ____ Letter (PL)
___23. HOUSE   W. Place where Usher put his twin sister's body (FHU)
___24. PURLOINED   X. ____Lee; she lived in a kingdom by the sea
___25. USHER   Y. Narrator's ____ burned down, leaving figure of a cat and rope on one wall (BC)

Poe Stories Matching 2 Answer Key

A - 1.	BELLS	A. To the rhyming and chiming of the ____
H - 2.	LETTER	B. Masque of ____ Death (MRD)
W - 3.	VAULT	C. Condition of Madame L'Espanaye's corpse (RM)
D - 4.	GALLOWS	D. Narrator thought white on the second cat's breast looked like____
N - 5.	EBONY	E. Montresor said he could taste the wine if Fortunato were busy
I - 6.	FACSIMILE	F. The cat's name (BC)
G - 7.	RODERICK	G. Mr. Usher (FHU)
P - 8.	MAD	H. It was stolen (PL)
O - 9.	DUPIN	I. Dupin replaced the letter with a ____(PL)
K - 10.	COSTUMES	J. Murderer greeted them warmly (TTH)
R - 11.	GOTHIC	K. What people wore to the ball (MRD)
C - 12.	MUTILATED	L. How the old man died (TTH)
F - 13.	PLUTO	M. Dupin was the ____ (RM)
X - 14.	ANNABEL	N. Color of clock (MRD)
T - 15.	FOOD	O. The detective (RM)
M - 16.	DETECTIVE	P. Crazy (TTH)
S - 17.	WALLS	Q. Quoth the Raven '____'
L - 18.	SUFFOCATED	R. Kind of story with mansion, dark tombs beneath/inside; ominous setting, living corpse (FHU)
Q - 19.	NEVERMORE	S. They moved inward (PP)
J - 20.	POLICE	T. Narrator put this on the ropes (PP)
B - 21.	RED	U. Fall of the House of ____ (FHU)
E - 22.	LUCHESI	V. The ____ Letter (PL)
Y - 23.	HOUSE	W. Place where Usher put his twin sister's body (FHU)
V - 24.	PURLOINED	X. ____Lee; she lived in a kingdom by the sea
U - 25.	USHER	Y. Narrator's ____ burned down, leaving figure of a cat and rope on one wall (BC)

Poe Stories Matching 3

___ 1. BOOK
___ 2. DETECTIVE
___ 3. RECESS
___ 4. DUNGEON
___ 5. SAILOR
___ 6. EYE
___ 7. LEBON
___ 8. TROWEL
___ 9. CASK
___10. FLOOR
___11. VAULT
___12. CAT
___13. SUFFOCATED
___14. MADELINE
___15. HEART
___16. ESPANAYE
___17. LUCHESI
___18. BELLS
___19. DUPIN
___20. COSTUMES
___21. GALLOWS
___22. MASQUE
___23. GOTHIC
___24. RAVEN
___25. MONTRESOR

A. The Tell-Tale ____ (TTH)
B. The ourang-outang belonged to him (RM)
C. How the old man died (TTH)
D. The murderer put the corpse under the ____ boards (TTH)
E. Vulture ____ (TTH)
F. Setting for the story (PP)
G. Kind of story with mansion, dark tombs beneath/inside; ominous setting, living corpse (FHU)
H. Place where Usher put his twin sister's body (FHU)
I. ____ of Red Death (MRD)
J. ____ of Amontillado (CA)
K. He decided to kill Fortunato (CA)
L. What people wore to the ball (MRD)
M. Madame L'____ and Mademoiselle Camille L'____ (RM)
N. Narrator met Dupin looking for the same rare ____ (RM)
O. Narrator thought white on the second cat's breast looked like ____
P. Lady ____ (FHU)
Q. The detective (RM)
R. Sign of a mason (CA)
S. Montresor said he could taste the wine if Fortunato were busy
T. Quoth the ____ 'Nevermore'
U. Dupin was the ____ (RM)
V. The Black ____ (BC)
W. Person accused of murders in Rue St. Morgue (RM)
X. Montresor bricked Fortunato into a ____ in the wall (CA)
Y. To the rhyming and chiming of the ____

Poe Stories Matching 3 Answer Key

N - 1. BOOK	A. The Tell-Tale ____ (TTH)
U - 2. DETECTIVE	B. The ourang-outang belonged to him (RM)
X - 3. RECESS	C. How the old man died (TTH)
F - 4. DUNGEON	D. The murderer put the corpse under the ____ boards (TTH)
B - 5. SAILOR	E. Vulture ____ (TTH)
E - 6. EYE	F. Setting for the story (PP)
W - 7. LEBON	G. Kind of story with mansion, dark tombs beneath/inside; ominous setting, living corpse (FHU)
R - 8. TROWEL	H. Place where Usher put his twin sister's body (FHU)
J - 9. CASK	I. ____ of Red Death (MRD)
D - 10. FLOOR	J. ____ of Amontillado (CA)
H - 11. VAULT	K. He decided to kill Fortunato (CA)
V - 12. CAT	L. What people wore to the ball (MRD)
C - 13. SUFFOCATED	M. Madame L'____ and Mademoiselle Camille L'____ (RM)
P - 14. MADELINE	N. Narrator met Dupin looking for the same rare ____ (RM)
A - 15. HEART	O. Narrator thought white on the second cat's breast looked like ____
M - 16. ESPANAYE	P. Lady ____ (FHU)
S - 17. LUCHESI	Q. The detective (RM)
Y - 18. BELLS	R. Sign of a mason (CA)
Q - 19. DUPIN	S. Montresor said he could taste the wine if Fortunato were busy
L - 20. COSTUMES	T. Quoth the ____ 'Nevermore'
O - 21. GALLOWS	U. Dupin was the ____ (RM)
I - 22. MASQUE	V. The Black ____ (BC)
G - 23. GOTHIC	W. Person accused of murders in Rue St. Morgue (RM)
T - 24. RAVEN	X. Montresor bricked Fortunato into a ____ in the wall (CA)
K - 25. MONTRESOR	Y. To the rhyming and chiming of the ____

Poe Stories Matching 4

___ 1. LUCHESI A. Narrator wanted them to eat the ropes (PP)
___ 2. EYE B. Dupin replaced the letter with a ____ (PL)
___ 3. LEBON C. ____ Lee; she lived in a kingdom by the sea
___ 4. PROPSPERO D. The Tell-Tale ____ (TTH)
___ 5. TROWEL E. Crazy (TTH)
___ 6. RAVEN F. The Prince (MRD)
___ 7. MONTRESOR G. Person accused of murders in Rue St. Morgue (RM)
___ 8. GOTHIC H. Vulture ____ (TTH)
___ 9. ESPANAYE I. The Pit and The ____ (PP)
___10. BOOK J. Sign of a mason (CA)
___11. PLUTO K. Narrator put this on the ropes (PP)
___12. EBONY L. Mr. Usher (FHU)
___13. MAD M. The cat's name (BC)
___14. RECESS N. Kind of story with mansion, dark tombs beneath/inside; ominous setting, living corpse (FHU)
___15. ANNABEL O. He decided to kill Fortunato (CA)
___16. HEART P. Montresor bricked Fortunato into a ____ in the wall (CA)
___17. FOOD Q. Madame L'____ and Mademoiselle Camille L'____ (RM)
___18. RODERICK R. Cask of ____ (CA)
___19. AMONTILLADO S. Narrator's ____ burned down, leaving figure of a cat and rope on one wall (BC)
___20. DEATH T. Montresor said he could taste the wine if Fortunato were busy
___21. PENDULUM U. Narrator met Dupin looking for the same rare ____ (RM)
___22. FACSIMILE V. Color of clock (MRD)
___23. CHAIR W. Quoth the ____ 'Nevermore'
___24. RATS X. Murderer placed his ____ over the place where he put the corpse
___25. HOUSE Y. Red ____; a highly contagious disease (MRD)

Poe Stories Matching 4 Answer Key

T - 1.	LUCHESI	A. Narrator wanted them to eat the ropes (PP)
H - 2.	EYE	B. Dupin replaced the letter with a ____ (PL)
G - 3.	LEBON	C. ____ Lee; she lived in a kingdom by the sea
F - 4.	PROPSPERO	D. The Tell-Tale ____ (TTH)
J - 5.	TROWEL	E. Crazy (TTH)
W - 6.	RAVEN	F. The Prince (MRD)
O - 7.	MONTRESOR	G. Person accused of murders in Rue St. Morgue (RM)
N - 8.	GOTHIC	H. Vulture ____ (TTH)
Q - 9.	ESPANAYE	I. The Pit and The ____ (PP)
U - 10.	BOOK	J. Sign of a mason (CA)
M - 11.	PLUTO	K. Narrator put this on the ropes (PP)
V - 12.	EBONY	L. Mr. Usher (FHU)
E - 13.	MAD	M. The cat's name (BC)
P - 14.	RECESS	N. Kind of story with mansion, dark tombs beneath/inside; ominous setting, living corpse (FHU)
C - 15.	ANNABEL	O. He decided to kill Fortunato (CA)
D - 16.	HEART	P. Montresor bricked Fortunato into a ____ in the wall (CA)
K - 17.	FOOD	Q. Madame L'____ and Mademoiselle Camille L'____ (RM)
L - 18.	RODERICK	R. Cask of ____ (CA)
R - 19.	AMONTILLADO	S. Narrator's ____ burned down, leaving figure of a cat and rope on one wall (BC)
Y - 20.	DEATH	T. Montresor said he could taste the wine if Fortunato were busy
I - 21.	PENDULUM	U. Narrator met Dupin looking for the same rare ____ (RM)
B - 22.	FACSIMILE	V. Color of clock (MRD)
X - 23.	CHAIR	W. Quoth the ____ 'Nevermore'
A - 24.	RATS	X. Murderer placed his ____ over the place where he put the corpse
S - 25.	HOUSE	Y. Red ____; a highly contagious disease (MRD)

Poe Stories Magic Squares 1

Match the definition with the vocabulary word. Put your answers in the magic squares below. When your answers are correct, all columns and rows will add to the same number.

A. GOTHIC
B. SUFFOCATED
C. LUCHESI
D. BELLS
E. MASQUE
F. CASK
G. REVENGE
H. USHER
I. RED
J. CHIMNEY
K. NEVERMORE
L. DUPIN
M. POLICE
N. EYE
O. TWIN
P. EBONY

1. Murderer greeted them warmly (TTH)
2. ____ of Amontillado (CA)
3. Fall of the House of ____ (FHU)
4. Usher put his ____ sister's body in a vault (FHU)
5. The detective (RM)
6. Montresor said he could taste the wine if Fortunato were busy
7. Kind of story with mansion, dark tombs beneath/inside; ominous setting, living corpse (FHU)
8. Place narrator disposed of his wife's body (BC)
9. Quoth the Raven '____'
10. To the rhyming and chiming of the ____
11. How the old man died (TTH)
12. Masque of ____ Death (MRD)
13. Vulture___(TTH)
14. ____ of Red Death (MRD)
15. Montresor's motive (CA)
16. Color of clock (MRD)

A=	B=	C=	D=
E=	F=	G=	H=
I=	J=	K=	L=
M=	N=	O=	P=

Poe Stories Magic Squares 1 Answer Key

Match the definition with the vocabulary word. Put your answers in the magic squares below. When your answers are correct, all columns and rows will add to the same number.

A. GOTHIC
B. SUFFOCATED
C. LUCHESI
D. BELLS
E. MASQUE
F. CASK

G. REVENGE
H. USHER
I. RED
J. CHIMNEY
K. NEVERMORE
L. DUPIN

M. POLICE
N. EYE
O. TWIN
P. EBONY

1. Murderer greeted them warmly (TTH)
2. ____ of Amontillado (CA)
3. Fall of the House of ____ (FHU)
4. Usher put his ____ sister's body in a vault (FHU)
5. The detective (RM)
6. Montresor said he could taste the wine if Fortunato were busy
7. Kind of story with mansion, dark tombs beneath/inside; ominous setting, living corpse (FHU)
8. Place narrator disposed of his wife's body (BC)
9. Quoth the Raven '____'
10. To the rhyming and chiming of the ____
11. How the old man died (TTH)
12. Masque of ____ Death (MRD)
13. Vulture____(TTH)
14. ____ of Red Death (MRD)
15. Montresor's motive (CA)
16. Color of clock (MRD)

A=7	B=11	C=6	D=10
E=14	F=2	G=15	H=3
I=12	J=8	K=9	L=5
M=1	N=13	O=4	P=16

Poe Stories Magic Squares 2

Match the definition with the vocabulary word. Put your answers in the magic squares below. When your answers are correct, all columns and rows will add to the same number.

A. CASK
B. LEBON
C. TROWEL
D. SUFFOCATED
E. ROPE
F. MASQUE
G. RODERICK
H. CAT
I. RATS
J. NEVERMORE
K. HEART
L. RECESS
M. FACSIMILE
N. GALLOWS
O. PLUTO
P. PROPSPERO

1. ____ of Red Death (MRD)
2. Narrator wanted them to eat the ropes (PP)
3. The cat's name (BC)
4. How the old man died (TTH)
5. Dupin replaced the letter with a ____ (PL)
6. Person accused of murders in Rue St. Morgue (RM)
7. The Black ____ (BC)
8. The Tell-Tale ____ (TTH)
9. Sign of a mason (CA)
10. The Prince (MRD)
11. Quoth the Raven '____'
12. Narrator hanged his cat with one (BC)
13. Montresor bricked Fortunato into a ____ in the wall (CA)
14. Mr. Usher (FHU)
15. ____ of Amontillado (CA)
16. Narrator thought white on the second cat's breast looked like ____

A=	B=	C=	D=
E=	F=	G=	H=
I=	J=	K=	L=
M=	N=	O=	P=

Poe Stories Magic Squares 2 Answer Key

Match the definition with the vocabulary word. Put your answers in the magic squares below. When your answers are correct, all columns and rows will add to the same number.

A. CASK
B. LEBON
C. TROWEL
D. SUFFOCATED
E. ROPE
F. MASQUE
G. RODERICK
H. CAT
I. RATS
J. NEVERMORE
K. HEART
L. RECESS
M. FACSIMILE
N. GALLOWS
O. PLUTO
P. PROPSPERO

1. ____ of Red Death (MRD)
2. Narrator wanted them to eat the ropes (PP)
3. The cat's name (BC)
4. How the old man died (TTH)
5. Dupin replaced the letter with a ____ (PL)
6. Person accused of murders in Rue St. Morgue (RM)
7. The Black ____ (BC)
8. The Tell-Tale ____ (TTH)
9. Sign of a mason (CA)
10. The Prince (MRD)
11. Quoth the Raven '____'
12. Narrator hanged his cat with one (BC)
13. Montresor bricked Fortunato into a ____ in the wall (CA)
14. Mr. Usher (FHU)
15. ____ of Amontillado (CA)
16. Narrator thought white on the second cat's breast looked like____

A=15	B=6	C=9	D=4
E=12	F=1	G=14	H=7
I=2	J=11	K=8	L=13
M=5	N=16	O=3	P=10

Poe Stories Magic Squares 3

Match the definition with the vocabulary word. Put your answers in the magic squares below. When your answers are correct, all columns and rows will add to the same number.

A. MADELINE
B. SAILOR
C. CHAIR
D. RAVEN
E. PROPSPERO
F. POLICE

G. BOOK
H. RATS
I. CASK
J. SEVEN
K. FLOOR
L. GOTHIC

M. RODERICK
N. MONTRESOR
O. HOUSE
P. EYE

1. Narrator wanted them to eat the ropes (PP)
2. Lady _____ (FHU)
3. The ourang-outang belonged to him (RM)
4. Narrator met Dupin looking for the same rare____ (RM)
5. Number of rooms in use at the Prince's ball (MRD)
6. Narrator's _____ burned down, leaving figure of a cat and rope on one wall (BC)
7. Vulture___(TTH)
8. ____ of Amontillado (CA)
9. The murderer put the corpse under the ____ boards(TTH)
10. He decided to kill Fortunato (CA)
11. Mr. Usher (FHU)
12. Kind of story with mansion, dark tombs beneath/inside; ominous setting, living corpse (FHU)
13. The Prince (MRD)
14. Quoth the ____ 'Nevermore'
15. Murderer placed his ____ over the place where he put the corpse
16. Murderer greeted them warmly (TTH)

A=	B=	C=	D=
E=	F=	G=	H=
I=	J=	K=	L=
M=	N=	O=	P=

Poe Stories Magic Squares 3 Answer Key

Match the definition with the vocabulary word. Put your answers in the magic squares below. When your answers are correct, all columns and rows will add to the same number.

A. MADELINE
B. SAILOR
C. CHAIR
D. RAVEN
E. PROPSPERO
F. POLICE

G. BOOK
H. RATS
I. CASK
J. SEVEN
K. FLOOR
L. GOTHIC

M. RODERICK
N. MONTRESOR
O. HOUSE
P. EYE

1. Narrator wanted them to eat the ropes (PP)
2. Lady ____ (FHU)
3. The ourang-outang belonged to him (RM)
4. Narrator met Dupin looking for the same rare____ (RM)
5. Number of rooms in use at the Prince's ball (MRD)
6. Narrator's ____ burned down, leaving figure of a cat and rope on one wall (BC)
7. Vulture___(TTH)
8. ____ of Amontillado (CA)
9. The murderer put the corpse under the ____ boards(TTH)
10. He decided to kill Fortunato (CA)
11. Mr. Usher (FHU)
12. Kind of story with mansion, dark tombs beneath/inside; ominous setting, living corpse (FHU)
13. The Prince (MRD)
14. Quoth the ____ 'Nevermore'
15. Murderer placed his ____ over the place where he put the corpse
16. Murderer greeted them warmly (TTH)

A=2	B=3	C=15	D=14
E=13	F=16	G=4	H=1
I=8	J=5	K=9	L=12
M=11	N=10	O=6	P=7

Poe Stories Magic Squares 4

Match the definition with the vocabulary word. Put your answers in the magic squares below. When your answers are correct, all columns and rows will add to the same number.

A. DUNGEON
B. GALLOWS
C. ANNABEL
D. WALLS
E. AXE
F. BOOK
G. USHER
H. FACSIMILE
I. PROPSPERO
J. PLUTO
K. MAD
L. MONTRESOR
M. DUPIN
N. PENDULUM
O. TROWEL
P. ESPANAYE

1. Narrator thought white on the second cat's breast looked like____
2. Fall of the House of ____ (FHU)
3. Crazy (TTH)
4. The Pit and The ____ (PP)
5. The detective (RM)
6. He decided to kill Fortunato (CA)
7. Dupin replaced the letter with a ____ (PL)
8. Setting for the story (PP)
9. Madame L'____ and Mademoiselle Camille L' ____ (RM)
10. The Prince (MRD)
11. Narrator murdered his wife with one (BC)
12. They moved inward (PP)
13. ____Lee; she lived in a kingdom by the sea
14. Narrator met Dupin looking for the same rare____ (RM)
15. The cat's name (BC)
16. Sign of a mason (CA)

A=	B=	C=	D=
E=	F=	G=	H=
I=	J=	K=	L=
M=	N=	O=	P=

Poe Stories Magic Squares 4 Answer Key

Match the definition with the vocabulary word. Put your answers in the magic squares below. When your answers are correct, all columns and rows will add to the same number.

A. DUNGEON
B. GALLOWS
C. ANNABEL
D. WALLS
E. AXE
F. BOOK
G. USHER
H. FACSIMILE
I. PROPSPERO
J. PLUTO
K. MAD
L. MONTRESOR
M. DUPIN
N. PENDULUM
O. TROWEL
P. ESPANAYE

1. Narrator thought white on the second cat's breast looked like____
2. Fall of the House of ____ (FHU)
3. Crazy (TTH)
4. The Pit and The ____ (PP)
5. The detective (RM)
6. He decided to kill Fortunato (CA)
7. Dupin replaced the letter with a ____(PL)
8. Setting for the story (PP)
9. Madame L'____ and Mademoiselle Camille L' ____ (RM)
10. The Prince (MRD)
11. Narrator murdered his wife with one (BC)
12. They moved inward (PP)
13. ____Lee; she lived in a kingdom by the sea
14. Narrator met Dupin looking for the same rare____ (RM)
15. The cat's name (BC)
16. Sign of a mason (CA)

A=8	B=1	C=13	D=12
E=11	F=14	G=2	H=7
I=10	J=15	K=3	L=6
M=5	N=4	O=16	P=9

Poe Stories Word Search 1

Words are placed backwards, forward, diagonally, up and down. Clues listed below can help you find the words. Circle the hidden vocabulary words in the maze.

```
M U T I L A T E D S A I L O R A R R F
C H C B D E T E C T I V E B C M O E Y
H O P H F A C S I M I L E L S O P V Z
Z U S U I P R O S E R T N O M N E E T
T S Y T R M O R O D E R I C K T V N R
G E D N U L N L S W O L L A G I K G O
M Q E N P M O E I D C J E H Z L H E W
Y J A I Q J E I Y C R H D D E L Y P E
P I T W A L L S N E E K A N N A B E L
R Y H T C E P O T E Z M M I N D R Y Y
F A F R B N E T P R D T D A R O F T P
B H V O H G E D N L H F P U D G O U R
T D N E N L X V Z V U S R E P H O S O
T J T U N X A C E E E T R F S I D H P
A V D F G T I Z U R K V O T S E N E S
C A S K L H J Q K C M S L L E B E R P
D C S U T O S O X N T O B X C O V D E
V Q A O S A O N Z A R J R Y E N E P R
F V G P M B Z R R X H X R E R Y S W O
```

Cask of _____ (CA) (11)
Color of clock (MRD) (5)
Condition of Madame L'Espanaye's corpse (RM) (9)
Crazy (TTH) (3)
Dupin replaced the letter with a ____ (PL) (9)
Dupin was the ____ (RM) (9)
Fall of the House of ____ (FHU) (5)
He decided to kill Fortunato (CA) (9)
It was stolen (PL) (6)
Kind of story with mansion, dark tombs beneath/inside; ominous setting, living corpse (FHU) (6)
Lady ____ (FHU) (8)
Madame L'____ and Mademoiselle Camille L'____ (RM) (8)
Masque of ____ Death (MRD) (3)
Montresor bricked Fortunato into a ____ in the wall (CA) (6)
Montresor's motive (CA) (7)
Mr. Usher (FHU) (8)
Murderer greeted them warmly (TTH) (6)
Murderer placed his ____ over the place where he put the corpse (5)
Narrator hanged his cat with one (BC) (4)
Narrator met Dupin looking for the same rare____ (RM) (4)
Narrator murdered his wife with one (BC) (3)
Narrator put this on the ropes (PP) (4)
Narrator thought white on the second cat's breast looked like____ (7)
Narrator wanted them to eat the ropes (PP) (4)

Narrator's ____ burned down, leaving figure of a cat and rope on one wall (BC) (5)
Number of rooms in use at the Prince's ball (MRD) (5)
Person accused of murders in Rue St. Morgue (RM) (5)
Place narrator disposed of his wife's body (BC) (7)
Place where Usher put his twin sister's body (FHU) (5)
Quoth the Raven '____' (9)
Quoth the ____ 'Nevermore' (5)
Red ____; a highly contagious disease (MRD) (5)
Setting for the story (PP) (7)
Sign of a mason (CA) (6)
The Black ____ (BC) (3)
The Prince (MRD) (9)
The Tell-Tale ____ (TTH) (5)
The ____ Letter (PL) (9)
The ____ and The Pendulum (PP) (3)
The cat's name (BC) (5)
The detective (RM) (5)
The murderer put the corpse under the ____ boards (TTH) (5)
The ourang-outang belonged to him (RM) (6)
They moved inward (PP) (5)
To the rhyming and chiming of the ____ (5)
Usher put his ____ sister's body in a vault (FHU) (4)
Vulture____ (TTH) (3)
What people wore to the ball (MRD) (8)
____ of Amontillado (CA) (4)
____ of Red Death (MRD) (6)
____ Lee; she lived in a kingdom by the sea (7)

Poe Stories Word Search 1 Answer Key

Words are placed backwards, forward, diagonally, up and down. Clues listed below can help you find the words. Circle the hidden vocabulary words in the maze.

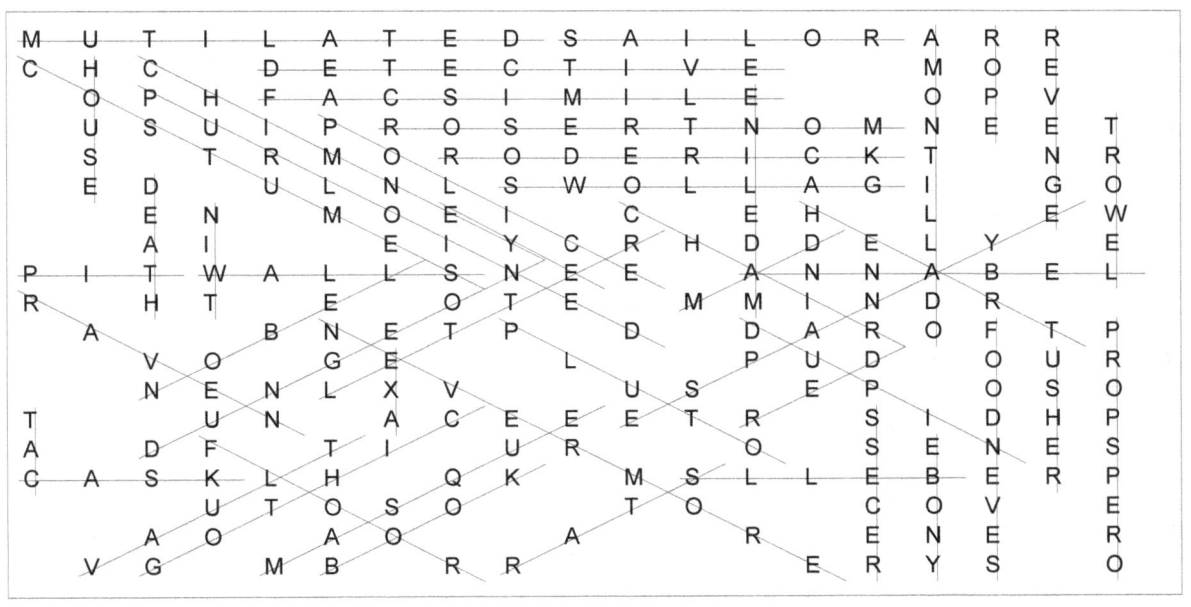

Cask of _____ (CA) (11)
Color of clock (MRD) (5)
Condition of Madame L'Espanaye's corpse (RM) (9)
Crazy (TTH) (3)
Dupin replaced the letter with a _____ (PL) (9)
Dupin was the _____ (RM) (9)
Fall of the House of _____ (FHU) (5)
He decided to kill Fortunato (CA) (9)
It was stolen (PL) (6)
Kind of story with mansion, dark tombs beneath/inside; ominous setting, living corpse (FHU) (6)
Lady _____ (FHU) (8)
Madame L'_____ and Mademoiselle Camille L' _____ (RM) (8)
Masque of _____ Death (MRD) (3)
Montresor bricked Fortunato into a _____ in the wall (CA) (6)
Montresor's motive (CA) (7)
Mr. Usher (FHU) (8)
Murderer greeted them warmly (TTH) (6)
Murderer placed his _____ over the place where he put the corpse (5)
Narrator hanged his cat with one (BC) (4)
Narrator met Dupin looking for the same rare_____ (RM) (4)
Narrator murdered his wife with one (BC) (3)
Narrator put this on the ropes (PP) (4)
Narrator thought white on the second cat's breast looked like_____ (7)
Narrator wanted them to eat the ropes (PP) (4)

Narrator's _____ burned down, leaving figure of a cat and rope on one wall (BC) (5)
Number of rooms in use at the Prince's ball (MRD) (5)
Person accused of murders in Rue St. Morgue (RM) (5)
Place narrator disposed of his wife's body (BC) (7)
Place where Usher put his twin sister's body (FHU) (5)
Quoth the Raven '_____' (9)
Quoth the _____ 'Nevermore' (5)
Red _____; a highly contagious disease (MRD) (5)
Setting for the story (PP) (7)
Sign of a mason (CA) (6)
The Black _____ (BC) (3)
The Prince (MRD) (9)
The Tell-Tale _____ (TTH) (5)
The _____ Letter (PL) (9)
The _____ and The Pendulum (PP) (3)
The cat's name (BC) (5)
The detective (RM) (5)
The murderer put the corpse under the _____ boards (TTH) (5)
The ourang-outang belonged to him (RM) (6)
They moved inward (PP) (5)
To the rhyming and chiming of the _____ (5)
Usher put his _____ sister's body in a vault (FHU) (4)
Vulture___(TTH) (3)
What people wore to the ball (MRD) (8)
_____ of Amontillado (CA) (4)
_____ of Red Death (MRD) (6)
_____Lee; she lived in a kingdom by the sea (7)

Poe Stories Word Search 2

Words are placed backwards, forward, diagonally, up and down. Clues listed below can help you find the words. Circle the hidden vocabulary words in the maze.

```
T R O W E L U S H E R N K A I M D H G
P O L I C E T K Z Y E M M S X E Z T A
M O N T R E S O R V S O E R U E N A L
V A U L T R B S A Y N H B Q Y F Y E L
H E A R T S E R L T C S S A C D G D O
P S X K L M V F I U B A N G W N X T W
B A P C U Y S L L M M A B Q E T M B S
L I R T M M L C Y O P X C V K M W A P
F L S O A A L P A S O R E A U M A X U
B O O K D R E C E S S R E T T E L E R
C R O O T E B N V N K E I D P N L B L
R Y X D X W R T I D D L V T C I S O O
A P J H L L I I T P A U K E M L D N I
T I P E Y E G N C T L N L I N E U Y N
S J P S C B O P E K O U S U W D N D E
M O Y U C A T D T B X C T X M A G U D
R H C O T N H B E G A Q H O K M E P C
R B Q H B N I L D F C H A I R S O I H
C F F C R A C H I M N E Y W R B N N Z
```

Cask of _____(CA) (11)
Color of clock (MRD) (5)
Condition of Madame L'Espanaye's corpse (RM) (9)
Crazy (TTH) (3)
Dupin replaced the letter with a ____(PL) (9)
Dupin was the ____ (RM) (9)
Fall of the House of ____ (FHU) (5)
He decided to kill Fortunato (CA) (9)
It was stolen (PL) (6)
Kind of story with mansion, dark tombs beneath/inside; ominous setting, living corpse (FHU) (6)
Lady ____ (FHU) (8)
Madame L'____ and Mademoiselle Camille L' ____ (RM) (8)
Masque of ____ Death (MRD) (3)
Montresor bricked Fortunato into a ____ in the wall (CA) (6)
Montresor said he could taste the wine if Fortunato were busy (7)
Montresor's motive (CA) (7)
Mr. Usher (FHU) (8)
Murderer greeted them warmly (TTH) (6)
Murderer placed his ____ over the place where he put the corpse (5)
Narrator hanged his cat with one (BC) (4)
Narrator met Dupin looking for the same rare____ (RM) (4)
Narrator murdered his wife with one (BC) (3)
Narrator put this on the ropes (PP) (4)
Narrator thought white on the second cat's breast looked like____ (7)
Narrator wanted them to eat the ropes (PP) (4)
Narrator's ____ burned down, leaving figure of a cat and rope on one wall (BC) (5)
Number of rooms in use at the Prince's ball (MRD) (5)
Person accused of murders in Rue St. Morgue (RM) (5)
Place narrator disposed of his wife's body (BC) (7)
Place where Usher put his twin sister's body (FHU) (5)
Quoth the ____ 'Nevermore' (5)
Red ____; a highly contagious disease (MRD) (5)
Setting for the story (PP) (7)
Sign of a mason (CA) (6)
The Black ____ (BC) (3)
The Pit and The ____ (PP) (8)
The Tell-Tale ____ (TTH) (5)
The ____ Letter (PL) (9)
The ____ and The Pendulum (PP) (3)
The cat's name (BC) (5)
The detective (RM) (5)
The murderer put the corpse under the ____ boards(TTH) (5)
The ourang-outang belonged to him (RM) (6)
They moved inward (PP) (5)
To the rhyming and chiming of the ____ (5)
Usher put his ____ sister's body in a vault (FHU) (4)
Vulture____(TTH) (3)
What people wore to the ball (MRD) (8)
____ of Amontillado (CA) (4)
____ of Red Death (MRD) (6)
____Lee; she lived in a kingdom by the sea (7)

Poe Stories Word Search 2 Answer Key

Words are placed backwards, forward, diagonally, up and down. Clues listed below can help you find the words. Circle the hidden vocabulary words in the maze.

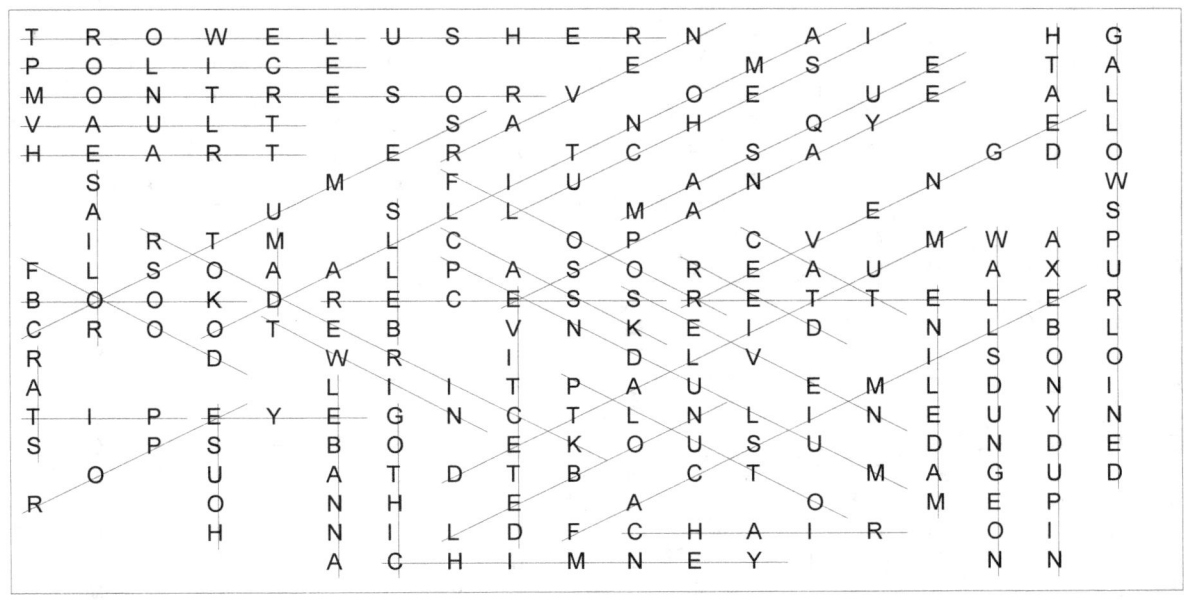

Cask of _____ (CA) (11)
Color of clock (MRD) (5)
Condition of Madame L'Espanaye's corpse (RM) (9)
Crazy (TTH) (3)
Dupin replaced the letter with a _____ (PL) (9)
Dupin was the _____ (RM) (9)
Fall of the House of _____ (FHU) (5)
He decided to kill Fortunato (CA) (9)
It was stolen (PL) (6)
Kind of story with mansion, dark tombs beneath/inside; ominous setting, living corpse (FHU) (6)
Lady _____ (FHU) (8)
Madame L'_____ and Mademoiselle Camille L' _____ (RM) (8)
Masque of _____ Death (MRD) (3)
Montresor bricked Fortunato into a _____ in the wall (CA) (6)
Montresor said he could taste the wine if Fortunato were busy (7)
Montresor's motive (CA) (7)
Mr. Usher (FHU) (8)
Murderer greeted them warmly (TTH) (6)
Murderer placed his _____ over the place where he put the corpse (5)
Narrator hanged his cat with one (BC) (4)
Narrator met Dupin looking for the same rare_____ (RM) (4)
Narrator murdered his wife with one (BC) (3)
Narrator put this on the ropes (PP) (4)
Narrator thought white on the second cat's breast looked like_____ (7)
Narrator wanted them to eat the ropes (PP) (4)
Narrator's _____ burned down, leaving figure of a cat and rope on one wall (BC) (5)
Number of rooms in use at the Prince's ball (MRD) (5)
Person accused of murders in Rue St. Morgue (RM) (5)
Place narrator disposed of his wife's body (BC) (7)
Place where Usher put his twin sister's body (FHU) (5)
Quoth the _____ 'Nevermore' (5)
Red _____; a highly contagious disease (MRD) (5)
Setting for the story (PP) (7)
Sign of a mason (CA) (6)
The Black _____ (BC) (3)
The Pit and The _____ (PP) (8)
The Tell-Tale _____ (TTH) (5)
The _____ Letter (PL) (9)
The _____ and The Pendulum (PP) (3)
The cat's name (BC) (5)
The detective (RM) (5)
The murderer put the corpse under the _____ boards (TTH) (5)
The ourang-outang belonged to him (RM) (6)
They moved inward (PP) (5)
To the rhyming and chiming of the _____ (5)
Usher put his _____ sister's body in a vault (FHU) (4)
Vulture_____ (TTH) (3)
What people wore to the ball (MRD) (8)
_____ of Amontillado (CA) (4)
_____ of Red Death (MRD) (6)
_____ Lee; she lived in a kingdom by the sea (7)

Poe Stories Word Search 3

Words are placed backwards, forward, diagonally, up and down. Words listed below are included in the maze. Circle the hidden vocabulary words in the maze.

```
D U N G E O N N C N E V E R M O R E V
M E G T F B N R D H R C E H K V J C N
M P A L N T I A E S I N B E H A Y A J
S L B T R K P T D E M O C Y X P S Y
H U M H H O U S E S P A N A Y E C K M
W C F B Y W D R C V O U Y E N N A S R
P H P F O Z W H T A R Y R D Y K T L K
S E O C O O C C I U P Z U L Q P L L H
Q S L H H C K I V L L M R O L I A S
C I I A Z B A H E T U F U A Q I Z W W
P T C I L E Y T D M T X T Q D X N N K
R R E R L L H O E Z O S I S L J W E V
E A O T Z L D G T D T K L R E H S U D
C N V P G S K I O R C Y A O T V H P J
E N M E S T P O O I D K T S T R E E C
S A W P N P F W R G S H E E E E A N M
S B Q Z Z F E E C A V W D R R V R I C
V E C F W L D R Z L R P N T G E T L N
L L L Q X O N S O L H Q S N N N M E J
S F T E R O B V P O V F V O F G A D M
H T W R B R W P R W X N N M S E S A K
M Q I Y M O W C O S T U M E S W Q M T
G J N Y Q X N F A C S I M I L E U P L
A M O N T I L L A D O R Z F Z B E P R
```

AMONTILLADO	DETECTIVE	HEART	PENDULUM	RODERICK
ANNABEL	DUNGEON	HOUSE	PIT	ROPE
AXE	DUPIN	LEBON	PLUTO	SAILOR
BELLS	EBONY	LETTER	POLICE	SEVEN
BOOK	ESPANAYE	LUCHESI	PROPSPERO	SUFFOCATED
CASK	EYE	MAD	PURLOINED	TROWEL
CAT	FACSIMILE	MADELINE	RATS	TWIN
CHAIR	FLOOR	MASQUE	RAVEN	USHER
CHIMNEY	FOOD	MONTRESOR	RECESS	VAULT
COSTUMES	GALLOWS	MUTILATED	RED	WALLS
DEATH	GOTHIC	NEVERMORE	REVENGE	

Poe Stories Word Search 3 Answer Key

Words are placed backwards, forward, diagonally, up and down. Words listed below are included in the maze. Circle the hidden vocabulary words in the maze.

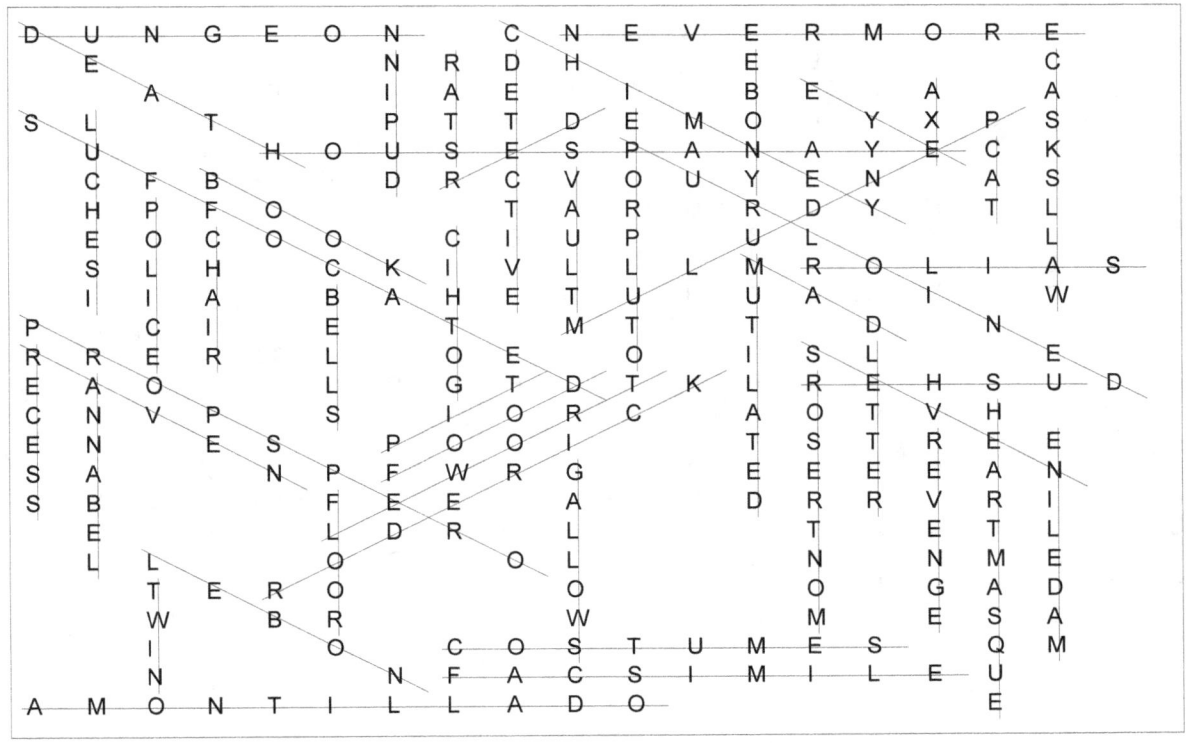

AMONTILLADO	DETECTIVE	HEART	PENDULUM	RODERICK
ANNABEL	DUNGEON	HOUSE	PIT	ROPE
AXE	DUPIN	LEBON	PLUTO	SAILOR
BELLS	EBONY	LETTER	POLICE	SEVEN
BOOK	ESPANAYE	LUCHESI	PROPSPERO	SUFFOCATED
CASK	EYE	MAD	PURLOINED	TROWEL
CAT	FACSIMILE	MADELINE	RATS	TWIN
CHAIR	FLOOR	MASQUE	RAVEN	USHER
CHIMNEY	FOOD	MONTRESOR	RECESS	VAULT
COSTUMES	GALLOWS	MUTILATED	RED	WALLS
DEATH	GOTHIC	NEVERMORE	REVENGE	

Poe Stories Word Search 4

Words are placed backwards, forward, diagonally, up and down. Words listed below are included in the maze. Circle the hidden vocabulary words in the maze.

```
H M M D W M P C W A L L S W O L L A G
O A U U L O E O V M L U Q R Y S F P A
U D T N R N S H G J C H X W F C U M
S E I G M T D T N D H G T D K J R O
E L L E M R U Y Y T E L L N F M L N
R I A O L E L M K Z M S P P K Q M O T
N N T N E S U E C V Q I X R B Y H I I
T E E S Y O M S U P R R D S B G N N L
P T D C A R D H S L Q B U U B D D E L
M H R R N R B P H U Y F X H P H T D A
N W S K A E R Y E T F Q M E T I D A D
M P R O P S P E R O W E X A P T N L O
X R R O S B S E C S L M E R S N X D X
Z O R E E C C A W I D D R T A Q Z E L
Y D T N Y E T X M F T L N B Z R U T V
N E V E S S E Q I V R E V E N G E C E
O R F S D Q S G O A N L V T H D A C V
B I P S Q C Y W Y T L W E F T V S T R
E C Z K A V E C J S D Y R P L E K I S
V K O F G L N H A A K A M O U O R V H
V O O V X D M A M T V V O L A B O E T
B O Y G V J I I C E P V R I V K L R D
D L E B O N H R N B T H E C T W I N J
G O T H I C C S A I L O R E D S V V N
```

AMONTILLADO   DETECTIVE   HEART   PENDULUM   RODERICK

ANNABEL   DUNGEON   HOUSE   PIT   ROPE

AXE   DUPIN   LEBON   PLUTO   SAILOR

BELLS   EBONY   LETTER   POLICE   SEVEN

BOOK   ESPANAYE   LUCHESI   PROPSPERO   SUFFOCATED

CASK   EYE   MAD   PURLOINED   TROWEL

CAT   FACSIMILE   MADELINE   RATS   TWIN

CHAIR   FLOOR   MASQUE   RAVEN   USHER

CHIMNEY   FOOD   MONTRESOR   RECESS   VAULT

COSTUMES   GALLOWS   MUTILATED   RED   WALLS

DEATH   GOTHIC   NEVERMORE   REVENGE

Poe Stories Word Search 4 Answer Key

Words are placed backwards, forward, diagonally, up and down. Words listed below are included in the maze. Circle the hidden vocabulary words in the maze.

AMONTILLADO	DETECTIVE	HEART	PENDULUM	RODERICK
ANNABEL	DUNGEON	HOUSE	PIT	ROPE
AXE	DUPIN	LEBON	PLUTO	SAILOR
BELLS	EBONY	LETTER	POLICE	SEVEN
BOOK	ESPANAYE	LUCHESI	PROPSPERO	SUFFOCATED
CASK	EYE	MAD	PURLOINED	TROWEL
CAT	FACSIMILE	MADELINE	RATS	TWIN
CHAIR	FLOOR	MASQUE	RAVEN	USHER
CHIMNEY	FOOD	MONTRESOR	RECESS	VAULT
COSTUMES	GALLOWS	MUTILATED	RED	WALLS
DEATH	GOTHIC	NEVERMORE	REVENGE	

Poe Stories Crossword 1

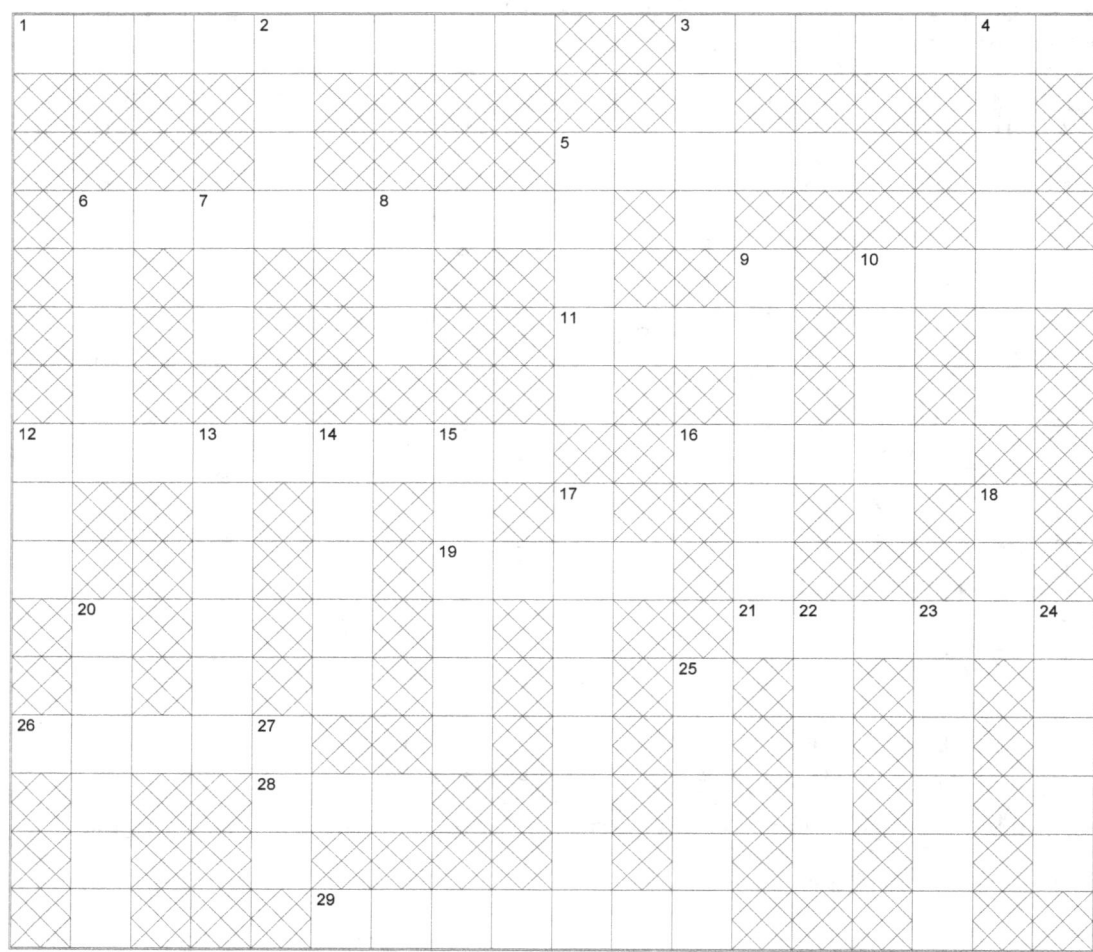

Across
1. Quoth the Raven '____'
3. Montresor's motive (CA)
5. The detective (RM)
6. Dupin replaced the letter with a ____(PL)
10. Narrator met Dupin looking for the same rare____ (RM)
11. Usher put his ____ sister's body in a vault (FHU)
12. The Prince (MRD)
16. They moved inward (PP)
19. ____ of Amontillado (CA)
21. It was stolen (PL)
26. Fall of the House of ____ (FHU)
28. Vulture___(TTH)
29. Setting for the story (PP)

Down
2. Narrator wanted them to eat the ropes (PP)
3. Narrator hanged his cat with one (BC)
4. Narrator thought white on the second cat's breast looked like____
5. Red ____; a highly contagious disease (MRD)
6. The murderer put the corpse under the ____ boards(TTH)
7. The Black ____ (BC)
8. Crazy (TTH)
9. ____Lee; she lived in a kingdom by the sea
10. To the rhyming and chiming of the ____
12. The ____ and The Pendulum (PP)
13. Murderer greeted them warmly (TTH)
14. The cat's name (BC)
15. Montresor bricked Fortunato into a ____ in the wall (CA)
17. Madame L'____ and Mademoiselle Camille L' ____ (RM)
18. Narrator murdered his wife with one (BC)
20. ____ of Red Death (MRD)
22. Color of clock (MRD)
23. Sign of a mason (CA)
24. Quoth the ____ 'Nevermore'
25. Number of rooms in use at the Prince's ball (MRD)
27. Masque of ____ Death (MRD)

Poe Stories Crossword 1 Answer Key

	1 N	E	V	2 E R	M	O	R	E		3 R	E	V	E	N	4 G	E
				A						O					A	
				T				5 D	U	P	I	N			L	
		6 F	7 A	C	8 S	I	M	I	L	E			9 A	10 B	O	O K
		L		A		A			A				A	B	O	K
		O		T			D		11 T	W	I	N		E		W
		O							H			N		L		S
12 P	R	13 O	P	14 S	P	15 E	R	O			16 W	A	L	L	S	
I		O		L		E			17 E		B		S		18 A	
T		L		U		19 C	A	S	K		E				X	
	20 M	I		T		E			P		21 L	22 E	23 T	T	24 E	R
	A		C		O		S		A		25 S	B	R		R	A
26 U	S	H	E	27 R		S			N		E	O	O		A	V
	Q			28 E	Y	E			A		V		N		W	E
	U			D					Y		E		Y		E	N
	E			29 D	U	N	G	E	O	N			L			

Across
1. Quoth the Raven '____'
3. Montresor's motive (CA)
5. The detective (RM)
6. Dupin replaced the letter with a ____(PL)
10. Narrator met Dupin looking for the same rare____ (RM)
11. Usher put his ____ sister's body in a vault (FHU)
12. The Prince (MRD)
16. They moved inward (PP)
19. ____ of Amontillado (CA)
21. It was stolen (PL)
26. Fall of the House of ____ (FHU)
28. Vulture___(TTH)
29. Setting for the story (PP)

Down
2. Narrator wanted them to eat the ropes (PP)
3. Narrator hanged his cat with one (BC)
4. Narrator thought white on the second cat's breast looked like____
5. Red ____; a highly contagious disease (MRD)
6. The murderer put the corpse under the ____ boards(TTH)
7. The Black ____ (BC)
8. Crazy (TTH)
9. ____Lee; she lived in a kingdom by the sea
10. To the rhyming and chiming of the ____
12. The ____ and The Pendulum (PP)
13. Murderer greeted them warmly (TTH)
14. The cat's name (BC)
15. Montresor bricked Fortunato into a ____ in the wall (CA)
17. Madame L'____ and Mademoiselle Camille L' ____ (RM)
18. Narrator murdered his wife with one (BC)
20. ____ of Red Death (MRD)
22. Color of clock (MRD)
23. Sign of a mason (CA)
24. Quoth the ____ 'Nevermore'
25. Number of rooms in use at the Prince's ball (MRD)
27. Masque of ____ Death (MRD)

Poe Stories Crossword 2

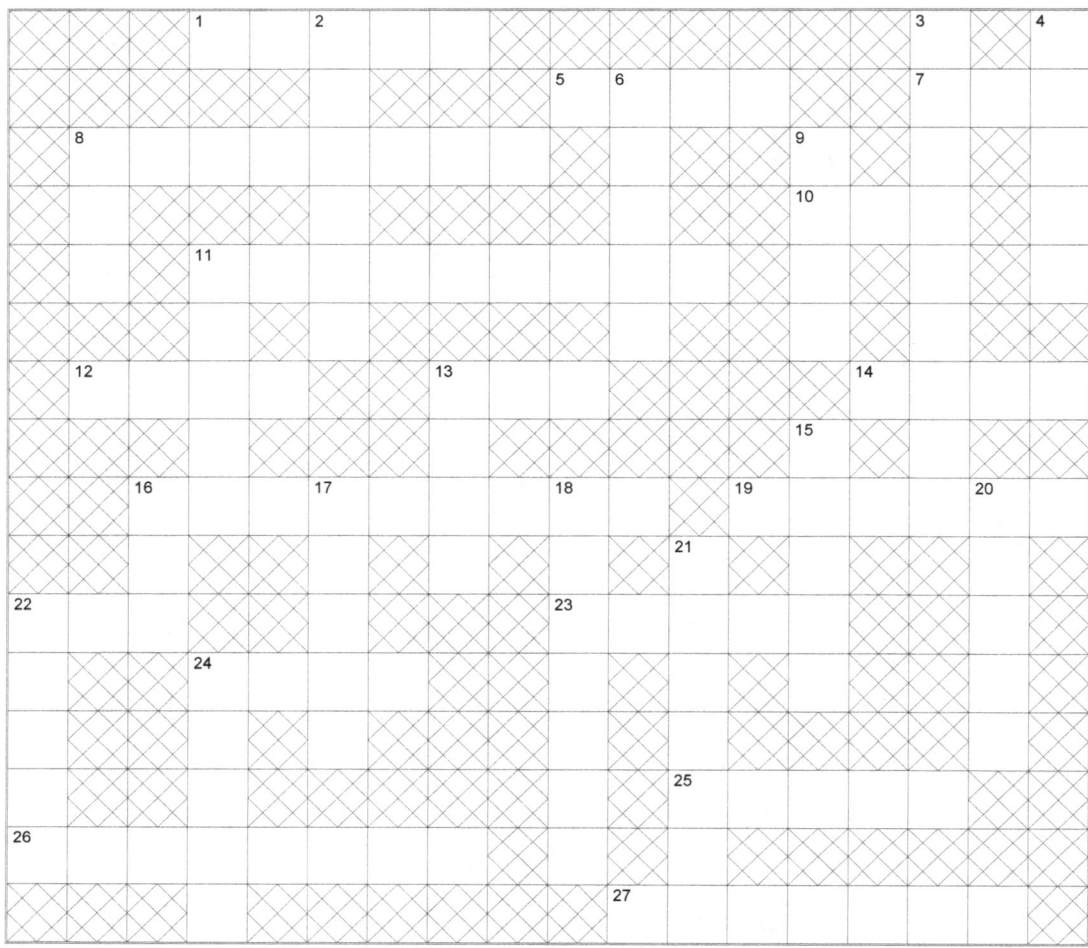

Across
1. The detective (RM)
5. Usher put his ____ sister's body in a vault (FHU)
7. Vulture____(TTH)
8. Lady ____ (FHU)
10. Narrator murdered his wife with one (BC)
11. Dupin replaced the letter with a ____(PL)
12. Narrator met Dupin looking for the same rare____ (RM)
13. Masque of ____ Death (MRD)
14. Narrator put this on the ropes (PP)
16. The Prince (MRD)
19. Montresor bricked Fortunato into a ____ in the wall (CA)
22. The Black ____ (BC)
23. Place where Usher put his twin sister's body (FHU)
24. Narrator wanted them to eat the ropes (PP)
25. Color of clock (MRD)
26. Mr. Usher (FHU)
27. ____Lee; she lived in a kingdom by the sea

Down
2. Murderer greeted them warmly (TTH)
3. Quoth the Raven '____'
4. To the rhyming and chiming of the ____
6. They moved inward (PP)
8. Crazy (TTH)
9. ____ of Amontillado (CA)
11. The murderer put the corpse under the ____ boards(TTH)
13. Narrator hanged his cat with one (BC)
15. Red ____; a highly contagious disease (MRD)
16. The ____ and The Pendulum (PP)
17. The cat's name (BC)
18. Montresor's motive (CA)
20. Number of rooms in use at the Prince's ball (MRD)
21. Setting for the story (PP)
22. Murderer placed his ____ over the place where he put the corpse
24. Quoth the ____ 'Nevermore'

Poe Stories Crossword 2 Answer Key

		1 D	U	2 P	I	N						3 N		4 B
				O				5 T	6 W	I	N		7 E	Y	E
	8 M	A	D	E	L	I	N	E		A		9 C	V		L
		A		I						L		10 A	X	E	L
		D		11 F	A	C	S	I	M	I	L	E		R	S
				L		E				S		K		M	
		12 B	O	O	K		13 R	E	D			14 F	O	O	D
				O			O				15 D		R		
			16 P	R	17 O	S	P	18 E	R	19 O	R	E	C	20 S	S
			I		L		E			21 D	A		E		
22 C	A	T			U			23 V	A	U	L	T		V	
H			24 R	A	T	S		E		N		H		E	
A			A		O			N		G				N	
I			V					G		25 E	B	O	N	Y	
26 R	O	D	E	R	I	C	K	E		O					
			N					27 A	N	N	A	B	E	L	

Across
1. The detective (RM)
5. Usher put his ____ sister's body in a vault (FHU)
7. Vulture___(TTH)
8. Lady ____ (FHU)
10. Narrator murdered his wife with one (BC)
11. Dupin replaced the letter with a ____(PL)
12. Narrator met Dupin looking for the same rare____ (RM)
13. Masque of ____ Death (MRD)
14. Narrator put this on the ropes (PP)
16. The Prince (MRD)
19. Montresor bricked Fortunato into a ____ in the wall (CA)
22. The Black ____ (BC)
23. Place where Usher put his twin sister's body (FHU)
24. Narrator wanted them to eat the ropes (PP)
25. Color of clock (MRD)
26. Mr. Usher (FHU)
27. ____Lee; she lived in a kingdom by the sea

Down
2. Murderer greeted them warmly (TTH)
3. Quoth the Raven '____'
4. To the rhyming and chiming of the ____
6. They moved inward (PP)
8. Crazy (TTH)
9. ____ of Amontillado (CA)
11. The murderer put the corpse under the ____ boards(TTH)
13. Narrator hanged his cat with one (BC)
15. Red ____; a highly contagious disease (MRD)
16. The ____ and The Pendulum (PP)
17. The cat's name (BC)
18. Montresor's motive (CA)
20. Number of rooms in use at the Prince's ball (MRD)
21. Setting for the story (PP)
22. Murderer placed his ____ over the place where he put the corpse
24. Quoth the ____ 'Nevermore'

Poe Stories Crossword 3

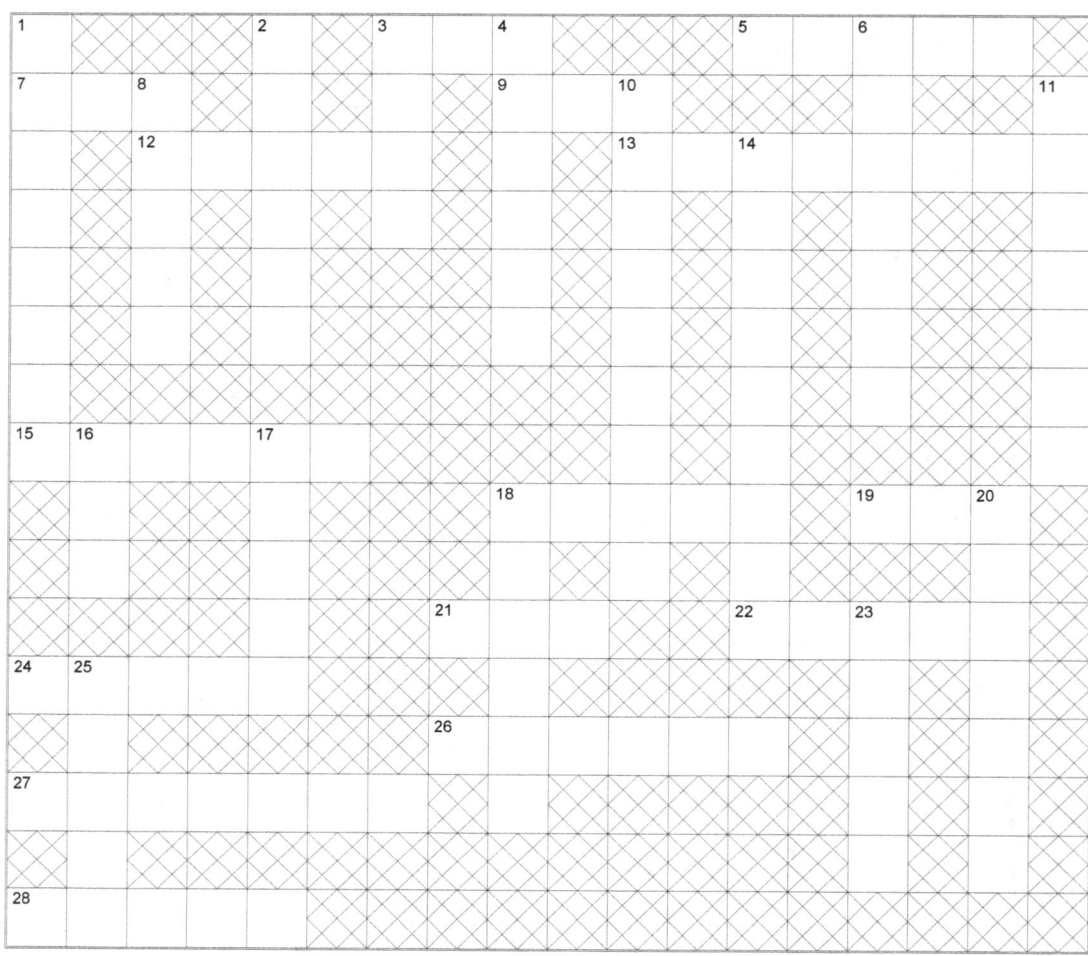

Across
3. The Black ____ (BC)
5. Red ____; a highly contagious disease (MRD)
7. Vulture____ (TTH)
9. Masque of ____ Death (MRD)
12. To the rhyming and chiming of the ____
13. Madame L'____ and Mademoiselle Camille L' ____ (RM)
15. ____ of Red Death (MRD)
18. Number of rooms in use at the Prince's ball (MRD)
19. Crazy (TTH)
21. The ____ and The Pendulum (PP)
22. The detective (RM)
24. Murderer placed his ____ over the place where he put the corpse
26. Kind of story with mansion, dark tombs beneath/inside; ominous setting, living corpse (FHU)
27. Montresor said he could taste the wine if Fortunato were busy
28. Person accused of murders in Rue St. Morgue (RM)

Down
1. The Pit and The ____ (PP)
2. Murderer greeted them warmly (TTH)
3. ____ of Amontillado (CA)
4. Sign of a mason (CA)
6. ____ Lee; she lived in a kingdom by the sea
8. Color of clock (MRD)
10. Dupin was the ____ (RM)
11. Montresor's motive (CA)
14. The ____ Letter (PL)
16. Narrator murdered his wife with one (BC)
17. Fall of the House of ____ (FHU)
18. The ourang-outang belonged to him (RM)
20. Setting for the story (PP)
23. The cat's name (BC)
25. Narrator's ____ burned down, leaving figure of a cat and rope on one wall (BC)

42
Copyrighted

Poe Stories Crossword 3 Answer Key

	1		2		3	4			5	6			
	P		P		C	A	T		D	E	A	T	H
7		8				9	10						11
E	Y	E	O		A	R	E	D			N		R
N		12					13	14					
N		B	E	L	L	S	O		E	S	P	A	N	A	Y	E
D		O		I		K		W		T	U		A			V
U		N		C				E		E	R		B			E
L		Y		E				L		C	L		E			N
U										T	O		L			G
15	16			17						I	I					E
M	A	S	Q	U	E			18					19	20		
	X			S				S	E	V	E	N		M	A	D
	E			H				A		E	E				U	
				E		21					22	23				
				E		P	I	T			D	U	P	I	N	
24	25															
C	H	A	I	R				L				L			G	
	O					26									E	
						G	O	T	H	I	C	U				
27																
L	U	C	H	E	S	I		R				T			O	
	S											O			N	
28																
L	E	B	O	N												

Across

3. The Black ____ (BC)
5. Red ____; a highly contagious disease (MRD)
7. Vulture ____ (TTH)
9. Masque of ____ Death (MRD)
12. To the rhyming and chiming of the ____
13. Madame L'____ and Mademoiselle Camille L'____ (RM)
15. ____ of Red Death (MRD)
18. Number of rooms in use at the Prince's ball (MRD)
19. Crazy (TTH)
21. The ____ and The Pendulum (PP)
22. The detective (RM)
24. Murderer placed his ____ over the place where he put the corpse
26. Kind of story with mansion, dark tombs beneath/inside; ominous setting, living corpse (FHU)
27. Montresor said he could taste the wine if Fortunato were busy
28. Person accused of murders in Rue St. Morgue (RM)

Down

1. The Pit and The ____ (PP)
2. Murderer greeted them warmly (TTH)
3. ____ of Amontillado (CA)
4. Sign of a mason (CA)
6. ____ Lee; she lived in a kingdom by the sea
8. Color of clock (MRD)
10. Dupin was the ____ (RM)
11. Montresor's motive (CA)
14. The ____ Letter (PL)
16. Narrator murdered his wife with one (BC)
17. Fall of the House of ____ (FHU)
18. The ourang-outang belonged to him (RM)
20. Setting for the story (PP)
23. The cat's name (BC)
25. Narrator's ____ burned down, leaving figure of a cat and rope on one wall (BC)

Poe Stories Crossword 4

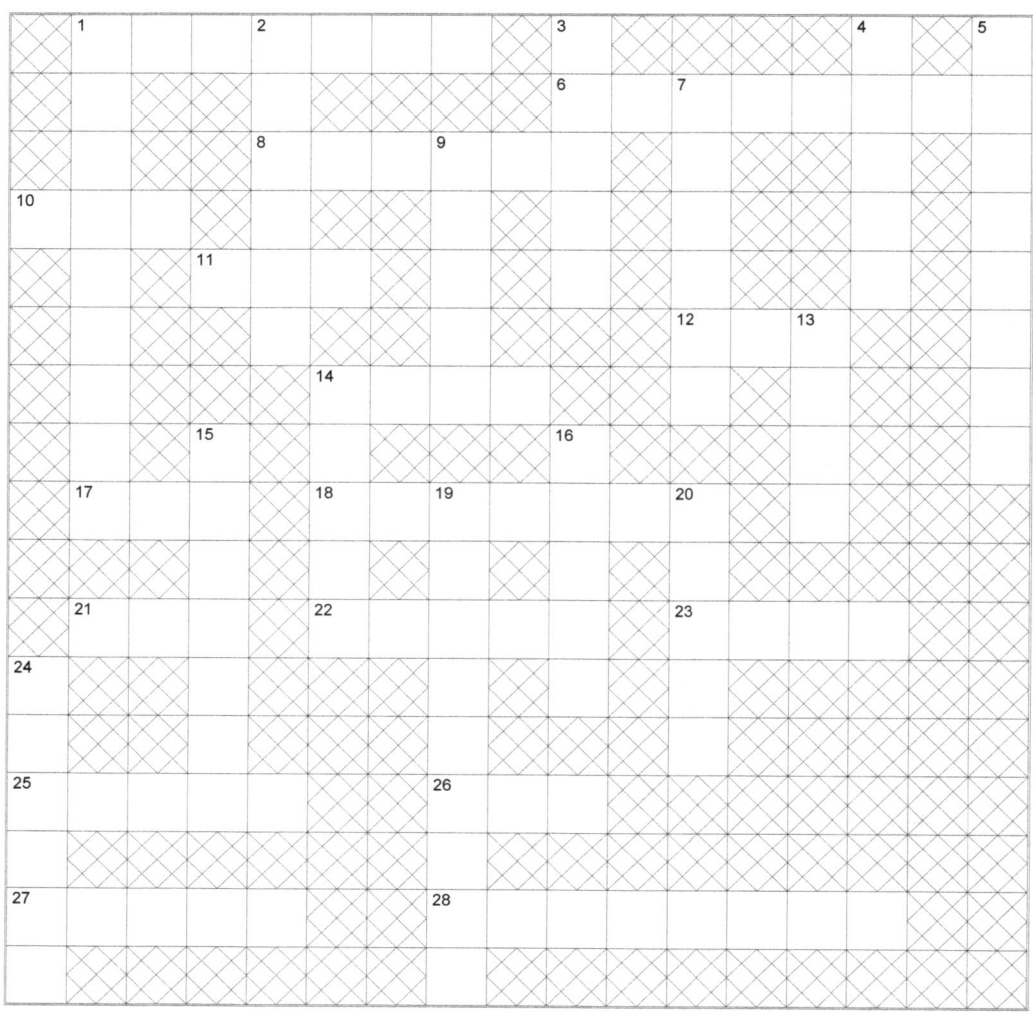

Across

1. Setting for the story (PP)
6. Madame L'____ and Mademoiselle Camille L' ____ (RM)
8. Sign of a mason (CA)
10. Masque of ____ Death (MRD)
11. The ____ and The Pendulum (PP)
12. The Black ____ (BC)
14. ____ of Amontillado (CA)
17. Vulture____ (TTH)
18. ____Lee; she lived in a kingdom by the sea
21. Narrator murdered his wife with one (BC)
22. Quoth the ____ 'Nevermore'
23. Narrator met Dupin looking for the same rare____ (RM)
25. Number of rooms in use at the Prince's ball (MRD)
26. Crazy (TTH)
27. Fall of the House of ____ (FHU)
28. Mr. Usher (FHU)

Down

1. Dupin was the ____ (RM)
2. Kind of story with mansion, dark tombs beneath/inside; ominous setting, living corpse (FHU)
3. To the rhyming and chiming of the ____
4. Place where Usher put his twin sister's body (FHU)
5. The Pit and The ____ (PP)
7. Murderer greeted them warmly (TTH)
9. They moved inward (PP)
13. Usher put his ____ sister's body in a vault (FHU)
14. Murderer placed his ____ over the place where he put the corpse
15. Montresor's motive (CA)
16. Color of clock (MRD)
19. Quoth the Raven '____'
20. Person accused of murders in Rue St. Morgue (RM)
24. ____ of Red Death (MRD)

44
Copyrighted

Poe Stories Crossword 4 Answer Key

	1 D	U	N	2 G	E	O	N		3 B				4 V		5 P
	E			O				6 E	S	7 P	A	N	A	Y	E
	T		8 T	R	O	W	9 E	L		O			U		N
10 R	E	D		H			A		L		L		L		D
	C		11 P	I	T		L		S		I		T		U
	T			C			L				12 C	13 A	T		L
	I				14 C	A	S	K		16 E	E	W			U
	V		15 R		H					E		I			M
	17 E	Y	E		18 A	19 N	N	A	B	20 E	L				
			V		I		E			O		E			
	21 A	X	E		22 R	A	V	E	N		23 B	O	O	K	
24 M			N				E		Y		O				
A			G				R				N				
25 S	E	V	E	N		26 M	A	D							
Q						O									
27 U	S	H	E	R		28 R	O	D	E	R	I	C	K		
E						E									

Across
1. Setting for the story (PP)
6. Madame L'____ and Mademoiselle Camille L'____ (RM)
8. Sign of a mason (CA)
10. Masque of ____ Death (MRD)
11. The ____ and The Pendulum (PP)
12. The Black ____ (BC)
14. ____ of Amontillado (CA)
17. Vulture___(TTH)
18. ____Lee; she lived in a kingdom by the sea
21. Narrator murdered his wife with one (BC)
22. Quoth the ____ 'Nevermore'
23. Narrator met Dupin looking for the same rare____ (RM)
25. Number of rooms in use at the Prince's ball (MRD)
26. Crazy (TTH)
27. Fall of the House of ____ (FHU)
28. Mr. Usher (FHU)

Down
1. Dupin was the ____ (RM)
2. Kind of story with mansion, dark tombs beneath/inside; ominous setting, living corpse (FHU)
3. To the rhyming and chiming of the ____
4. Place where Usher put his twin sister's body (FHU)
5. The Pit and The ____ (PP)
7. Murderer greeted them warmly (TTH)
9. They moved inward (PP)
13. Usher put his ____ sister's body in a vault (FHU)
14. Murderer placed his ____ over the place where he put the corpse
15. Montresor's motive (CA)
16. Color of clock (MRD)
19. Quoth the Raven '____'
20. Person accused of murders in Rue St. Morgue (RM)
24. ____ of Red Death (MRD)

Poe Stories

RAVEN	PURLOINED	BELLS	ANNABEL	PROPSPERO
RED	DUPIN	PLUTO	REVENGE	DEATH
MADELINE	COSTUMES	FREE SPACE	AXE	EYE
NEVERMORE	RECESS	SEVEN	DUNGEON	BOOK
MONTRESOR	LETTER	EBONY	SAILOR	ROPE

Poe Stories

SUFFOCATED	AMONTILLADO	RATS	FLOOR	DETECTIVE
USHER	FOOD	POLICE	CHAIR	PENDULUM
CHIMNEY	HEART	FREE SPACE	MAD	CAT
PIT	TWIN	TROWEL	ESPANAYE	FACSIMILE
LEBON	MUTILATED	MASQUE	WALLS	CASK

Poe Stories

LETTER	AXE	USHER	LUCHESI	HOUSE
PROPSPERO	MUTILATED	DUNGEON	GOTHIC	DUPIN
PLUTO	SEVEN	FREE SPACE	TWIN	CASK
ROPE	FLOOR	PURLOINED	RED	AMONTILLADO
WALLS	ANNABEL	EBONY	DETECTIVE	NEVERMORE

Poe Stories

RATS	TROWEL	PENDULUM	HEART	MADELINE
MASQUE	BELLS	SAILOR	SUFFOCATED	CHAIR
RECESS	MONTRESOR	FREE SPACE	REVENGE	BOOK
MAD	RAVEN	GALLOWS	POLICE	LEBON
RODERICK	CHIMNEY	DEATH	EYE	COSTUMES

Poe Stories

POLICE	PENDULUM	LUCHESI	EBONY	DUPIN
PLUTO	RATS	HOUSE	SEVEN	TROWEL
ANNABEL	CAT	FREE SPACE	WALLS	USHER
GOTHIC	COSTUMES	LEBON	DEATH	TWIN
GALLOWS	ESPANAYE	NEVERMORE	MADELINE	REVENGE

Poe Stories

BOOK	CHIMNEY	HEART	RAVEN	PURLOINED
RECESS	CASK	FLOOR	SAILOR	RODERICK
DUNGEON	PROPSPERO	FREE SPACE	SUFFOCATED	VAULT
MONTRESOR	DETECTIVE	EYE	PIT	ROPE
RED	FOOD	MAD	MUTILATED	CHAIR

Poe Stories

ROPE	TROWEL	SEVEN	MASQUE	FLOOR
TWIN	ESPANAYE	POLICE	GALLOWS	USHER
LUCHESI	EYE	FREE SPACE	PROPSPERO	PIT
NEVERMORE	RED	WALLS	DUNGEON	SAILOR
PENDULUM	LETTER	RODERICK	MADELINE	AXE

Poe Stories

BOOK	EBONY	MONTRESOR	CAT	DETECTIVE
FOOD	MUTILATED	HOUSE	BELLS	CHIMNEY
LEBON	DEATH	FREE SPACE	GOTHIC	PURLOINED
VAULT	SUFFOCATED	CASK	RATS	AMONTILLADO
DUPIN	RAVEN	ANNABEL	REVENGE	COSTUMES

Poe Stories

FLOOR	ESPANAYE	WALLS	NEVERMORE	TWIN
RAVEN	RATS	LEBON	SAILOR	VAULT
GALLOWS	RED	FREE SPACE	AXE	PENDULUM
ROPE	RODERICK	DETECTIVE	PLUTO	MUTILATED
USHER	COSTUMES	FOOD	MASQUE	HOUSE

Poe Stories

PURLOINED	DUNGEON	MONTRESOR	DEATH	POLICE
ANNABEL	CASK	TROWEL	LETTER	FACSIMILE
MAD	EYE	FREE SPACE	BELLS	PIT
CHAIR	RECESS	MADELINE	HEART	SEVEN
PROPSPERO	DUPIN	BOOK	REVENGE	CAT

Poe Stories

USHER	DUPIN	SAILOR	LUCHESI	AMONTILLADO
CHIMNEY	EYE	RAVEN	TWIN	PURLOINED
DUNGEON	LETTER	FREE SPACE	ROPE	MAD
HOUSE	BOOK	MONTRESOR	LEBON	PROPSPERO
FOOD	FACSIMILE	RECESS	BELLS	COSTUMES

Poe Stories

ANNABEL	CASK	SUFFOCATED	RODERICK	GOTHIC
MASQUE	GALLOWS	DEATH	RED	SEVEN
WALLS	PIT	FREE SPACE	VAULT	CAT
FLOOR	EBONY	PLUTO	REVENGE	POLICE
NEVERMORE	CHAIR	AXE	DETECTIVE	ESPANAYE

Poe Stories

MADELINE	TROWEL	RATS	CHAIR	ANNABEL
RECESS	RED	RAVEN	LETTER	DEATH
ROPE	MAD	FREE SPACE	CHIMNEY	AXE
GOTHIC	SEVEN	HOUSE	POLICE	AMONTILLADO
EYE	REVENGE	SAILOR	CASK	EBONY

Poe Stories

BOOK	PURLOINED	TWIN	LUCHESI	LEBON
PIT	FACSIMILE	RODERICK	CAT	PROPSPERO
ESPANAYE	SUFFOCATED	FREE SPACE	FLOOR	DETECTIVE
COSTUMES	PENDULUM	MUTILATED	USHER	PLUTO
DUNGEON	GALLOWS	FOOD	BELLS	WALLS

Poe Stories

MASQUE	FOOD	FACSIMILE	PROPSPERO	DETECTIVE
ANNABEL	DUPIN	TWIN	BOOK	HEART
ROPE	HOUSE	FREE SPACE	MONTRESOR	EBONY
MUTILATED	PENDULUM	RECESS	CASK	RAVEN
MADELINE	WALLS	CHIMNEY	AMONTILLADO	DUNGEON

Poe Stories

SUFFOCATED	RATS	BELLS	POLICE	PURLOINED
NEVERMORE	CHAIR	PLUTO	USHER	PIT
RODERICK	DEATH	FREE SPACE	ESPANAYE	VAULT
MAD	RED	GOTHIC	CAT	TROWEL
LETTER	EYE	COSTUMES	LUCHESI	AXE

Poe Stories

RODERICK	RATS	POLICE	BELLS	PURLOINED
PLUTO	PENDULUM	NEVERMORE	FACSIMILE	VAULT
LUCHESI	AMONTILLADO	FREE SPACE	ESPANAYE	GALLOWS
CHAIR	DEATH	ROPE	CASK	HEART
WALLS	PIT	LEBON	MADELINE	TROWEL

Poe Stories

COSTUMES	USHER	PROPSPERO	FLOOR	SEVEN
EYE	DUPIN	RECESS	ANNABEL	LETTER
MAD	SAILOR	FREE SPACE	CHIMNEY	CAT
MUTILATED	HOUSE	DUNGEON	MONTRESOR	AXE
REVENGE	EBONY	RAVEN	GOTHIC	MASQUE

Poe Stories

TWIN	HEART	GALLOWS	DETECTIVE	MAD
PLUTO	PENDULUM	MADELINE	SEVEN	FOOD
PROPSPERO	RATS	FREE SPACE	BOOK	GOTHIC
LETTER	BELLS	DUNGEON	PURLOINED	RODERICK
CAT	SUFFOCATED	ESPANAYE	AXE	COSTUMES

Poe Stories

RAVEN	TROWEL	DEATH	EBONY	PIT
RED	MASQUE	REVENGE	AMONTILLADO	MUTILATED
SAILOR	LUCHESI	FREE SPACE	FACSIMILE	MONTRESOR
VAULT	HOUSE	FLOOR	CHAIR	ROPE
LEBON	USHER	NEVERMORE	DUPIN	WALLS

Poe Stories

FLOOR	RATS	TWIN	REVENGE	DETECTIVE
LETTER	TROWEL	SUFFOCATED	GALLOWS	FOOD
PURLOINED	MONTRESOR	FREE SPACE	WALLS	CAT
AMONTILLADO	USHER	DEATH	MASQUE	LEBON
POLICE	CHIMNEY	GOTHIC	NEVERMORE	RED

Poe Stories

PROPSPERO	ROPE	CASK	RECESS	SEVEN
HEART	AXE	EYE	DUPIN	VAULT
CHAIR	RAVEN	FREE SPACE	SAILOR	MUTILATED
LUCHESI	HOUSE	MADELINE	COSTUMES	ANNABEL
EBONY	BELLS	ESPANAYE	DUNGEON	PIT

Poe Stories

SUFFOCATED	SAILOR	MUTILATED	ESPANAYE	TROWEL
BOOK	NEVERMORE	VAULT	USHER	EYE
LETTER	AXE	FREE SPACE	DETECTIVE	PROPSPERO
PIT	CAT	HOUSE	MASQUE	RAVEN
DUNGEON	PENDULUM	CHAIR	GALLOWS	MONTRESOR

Poe Stories

ROPE	EBONY	DEATH	FLOOR	SEVEN
LEBON	WALLS	RED	POLICE	TWIN
GOTHIC	MADELINE	FREE SPACE	CHIMNEY	MAD
RECESS	PLUTO	COSTUMES	AMONTILLADO	BELLS
ANNABEL	LUCHESI	RATS	HEART	PURLOINED

Poe Stories

ESPANAYE	COSTUMES	MASQUE	GOTHIC	RAVEN
TWIN	FOOD	SUFFOCATED	LUCHESI	GALLOWS
DEATH	AXE	FREE SPACE	POLICE	SAILOR
MAD	ROPE	PLUTO	DUNGEON	CAT
EYE	MONTRESOR	LETTER	VAULT	HOUSE

Poe Stories

TROWEL	PROPSPERO	WALLS	PURLOINED	AMONTILLADO
HEART	FACSIMILE	NEVERMORE	ANNABEL	PIT
CHIMNEY	PENDULUM	FREE SPACE	CHAIR	CASK
SEVEN	DUPIN	FLOOR	MADELINE	RODERICK
REVENGE	EBONY	RECESS	DETECTIVE	RED

Poe Stories

BELLS	RED	LEBON	RECESS	MADELINE
PLUTO	PIT	CAT	RAVEN	FLOOR
FACSIMILE	RATS	FREE SPACE	MAD	BOOK
ANNABEL	PURLOINED	TROWEL	SAILOR	MASQUE
HOUSE	DUNGEON	MUTILATED	RODERICK	SEVEN

Poe Stories

FOOD	SUFFOCATED	DUPIN	HEART	POLICE
DEATH	USHER	PENDULUM	LETTER	GOTHIC
AXE	COSTUMES	FREE SPACE	TWIN	ROPE
CASK	VAULT	NEVERMORE	ESPANAYE	AMONTILLADO
LUCHESI	EYE	PROPSPERO	DETECTIVE	GALLOWS

Poe Stories

MONTRESOR	CHAIR	LETTER	VAULT	CAT
WALLS	ROPE	POLICE	RED	ESPANAYE
BOOK	PURLOINED	FREE SPACE	SEVEN	MUTILATED
SUFFOCATED	REVENGE	MASQUE	DUNGEON	FLOOR
LUCHESI	DUPIN	COSTUMES	LEBON	PENDULUM

Poe Stories

TWIN	PROPSPERO	GOTHIC	DEATH	MADELINE
EBONY	GALLOWS	BELLS	HOUSE	ANNABEL
TROWEL	RAVEN	FREE SPACE	RODERICK	HEART
USHER	DETECTIVE	CHIMNEY	RATS	FOOD
FACSIMILE	SAILOR	MAD	RECESS	AXE

Poe Stories

REVENGE	NEVERMORE	ROPE	LEBON	AMONTILLADO
FLOOR	SAILOR	VAULT	RAVEN	EYE
FACSIMILE	TWIN	FREE SPACE	GALLOWS	CHIMNEY
GOTHIC	WALLS	SUFFOCATED	POLICE	TROWEL
SEVEN	RATS	DEATH	CAT	ANNABEL

Poe Stories

USHER	PLUTO	DUNGEON	EBONY	FOOD
PURLOINED	RED	BELLS	ESPANAYE	MADELINE
MUTILATED	DETECTIVE	FREE SPACE	MAD	RODERICK
MONTRESOR	HEART	PENDULUM	LUCHESI	PIT
CHAIR	DUPIN	COSTUMES	RECESS	HOUSE

Poe Stories Vocabulary Word List

No.	Word	Clue/Definition
1.	AMID	In the middle of
2.	ANNIHILATE	To reduce to nonexistence; to nullify or render void; abolish
3.	APPARITION	A ghostly figure
4.	ASCERTAIN	To find out
5.	ASTUTE	Shrewd
6.	ASUNDER	Into separate parts or pieces
7.	AUDACITY	Boldness; daring
8.	BEGUILING	Deceiving; diverting
9.	COGNIZANT	Aware; familiar with
10.	CONCEIVED	To form or develop in the mind; devise
11.	CONSIGNED	Handed over
12.	CORROBORATES	To strengthen or support with other evidence
13.	COUNTENANCES	Faces
14.	COVETED	Wished for longingly
15.	CULPABLE	Responsible; at fault
16.	DERISION	Scoffing; ridicule
17.	DISSIMULATION	Concealing one's true feelings or intentions
18.	ECSTATIC	Euphoric; blissful
19.	EGREGIOUS	Bad or offensive
20.	EGRESS	Exit; escape
21.	ENAMORED	Inspired; captivated
22.	EPOCH	Age; time
23.	IMPEDED	Obstructed
24.	IMPUNITY	Exemption from punishment, penalty, or harm
25.	IRREVOCABLE	Can't be turned back
26.	LIVID	Bruised
27.	LUCID	Easily understood; sane or rational
28.	MALEVOLENCE	Ill will toward other; rancor; malice; evil influence, especially supernatural
29.	MANIFOLD	One of may kinds
30.	MIEN	Manner
31.	NEBULOUS	Cloudy, misty, or hazy
32.	ODIOUS	Evoking feelings of repulsion
33.	ORBS	Eyes
34.	PALLID	Pale; dull
35.	PERVERSENESS	Quality of being directed away from what is right or good; an appalling action, situation or object
36.	PRODIGIOUS	Enormous
37.	PROMISCUOUSLY	Causally; randomly
38.	REQUIEM	A hymn, composition, or service for the dead
39.	SAGACIOUS	Wise
40.	SAGACITY	The quality of being discerning, sound in judgement
41.	SERE	Withered; dry
42.	SUBLIME	Majestic; inspiring awe; impressive
43.	SUCCUMBED	Gave in
44.	SULTRINESS	Sensualness; voluptuousness
45.	UNPERCEIVED	Unnoticed
46.	VEXED	To bring distress or suffering to; plague
47.	VORACITY	Wild hunger

Copyrighted

Poe Stories Vocabulary Fill In The Blanks 1

_____

_____

_____

_____

_____

_____

_____

_____

_____

_____

_____

_____

_____

_____

_____

_____

_____

_____

_____

_____

1. Deceiving; diverting
2. Exemption from punishment, penalty, or harm
3. A ghostly figure
4. Bad or offensive
5. Gave in
6. Ill will toward other; rancor; malice; evil influence, especially supernatural
7. Causally; randomly
8. Obstructed
9. A hymn, composition, or service for the dead
10. Faces
11. One of may kinds
12. To reduce to nonexistence; to nullify or render void; abolish
13. Quality of being directed away from what is right or good; an appalling action, situation or object
14. Manner
15. Concealing one's true feelings or intentions
16. Can't be turned back
17. Age; time
18. Enormous
19. Handed over
20. Shrewd

Poe Stories Vocabulary Fill In The Blanks 1 Answer Key

BEGUILING	1. Deceiving; diverting
IMPUNITY	2. Exemption from punishment, penalty, or harm
APPARITION	3. A ghostly figure
EGREGIOUS	4. Bad or offensive
SUCCUMBED	5. Gave in
MALEVOLENCE	6. Ill will toward other; rancor; malice; evil influence, especially supernatural
PROMISCUOUSLY	7. Causally; randomly
IMPEDED	8. Obstructed
REQUIEM	9. A hymn, composition, or service for the dead
COUNTENANCES	10. Faces
MANIFOLD	11. One of may kinds
ANNIHILATE	12. To reduce to nonexistence; to nullify or render void; abolish
PERVERSENESS	13. Quality of being directed away from what is right or good; an appalling action, situation or object
MIEN	14. Manner
DISSIMULATION	15. Concealing one's true feelings or intentions
IRREVOCABLE	16. Can't be turned back
EPOCH	17. Age; time
PRODIGIOUS	18. Enormous
CONSIGNED	19. Handed over
ASTUTE	20. Shrewd

Poe Stories Vocabulary Fill In The Blanks 2

1. Enormous
2. Sensualness; voluptuousness
3. To bring distress or suffering to; plague
4. Age; time
5. Pale; dull
6. Causally; randomly
7. Deceiving; diverting
8. Manner
9. Exit; escape
10. Faces
11. Can't be turned back
12. In the middle of
13. Concealing one's true feelings or intentions
14. A ghostly figure
15. Exemption from punishment, penalty, or harm
16. Euphoric; blissful
17. Eyes
18. Ill will toward other; rancor; malice; evil influence, especially supernatural
19. Boldness; daring
20. One of may kinds

Poe Stories Vocabulary Fill In The Blanks 2 Answer Key

PRODIGIOUS	1. Enormous
SULTRINESS	2. Sensualness; voluptuousness
VEXED	3. To bring distress or suffering to; plague
EPOCH	4. Age; time
PALLID	5. Pale; dull
PROMISCUOUSLY	6. Causally; randomly
BEGUILING	7. Deceiving; diverting
MIEN	8. Manner
EGRESS	9. Exit; escape
COUNTENANCES	10. Faces
IRREVOCABLE	11. Can't be turned back
AMID	12. In the middle of
DISSIMULATION	13. Concealing one's true feelings or intentions
APPARITION	14. A ghostly figure
IMPUNITY	15. Exemption from punishment, penalty, or harm
ECSTATIC	16. Euphoric; blissful
ORBS	17. Eyes
MALEVOLENCE	18. Ill will toward other; rancor; malice; evil influence, especially supernatural
AUDACITY	19. Boldness; daring
MANIFOLD	20. One of may kinds

Poe Stories Vocabulary Fill In The Blanks 3

_____ 1. Withered; dry

_____ 2. To find out

_____ 3. Manner

_____ 4. Quality of being directed away from what is right or good; an appalling action, situation or object

_____ 5. Bruised

_____ 6. Can't be turned back

_____ 7. A ghostly figure

_____ 8. Wise

_____ 9. Boldness; daring

_____ 10. Gave in

_____ 11. Scoffing; ridicule

_____ 12. Handed over

_____ 13. Faces

_____ 14. Responsible; at fault

_____ 15. Pale; dull

_____ 16. Aware; familiar with

_____ 17. Eyes

_____ 18. The quality of being discerning, sound in judgement

_____ 19. Cloudy, misty, or hazy

_____ 20. Wished for longingly

Poe Stories Vocabulary Fill In The Blanks 3 Answer Key

SERE	1. Withered; dry
ASCERTAIN	2. To find out
MIEN	3. Manner
PERVERSENESS	4. Quality of being directed away from what is right or good; an appalling action, situation or object
LIVID	5. Bruised
IRREVOCABLE	6. Can't be turned back
APPARITION	7. A ghostly figure
SAGACIOUS	8. Wise
AUDACITY	9. Boldness; daring
SUCCUMBED	10. Gave in
DERISION	11. Scoffing; ridicule
CONSIGNED	12. Handed over
COUNTENANCES	13. Faces
CULPABLE	14. Responsible; at fault
PALLID	15. Pale; dull
COGNIZANT	16. Aware; familiar with
ORBS	17. Eyes
SAGACITY	18. The quality of being discerning, sound in judgement
NEBULOUS	19. Cloudy, misty, or hazy
COVETED	20. Wished for longingly

Poe Stories Vocabulary Fill In The Blanks 4

_____ 1. Age; time

_____ 2. Responsible; at fault

_____ 3. A ghostly figure

_____ 4. Gave in

_____ 5. Wished for longingly

_____ 6. One of may kinds

_____ 7. To form or develop in the mind; devise

_____ 8. Euphoric; blissful

_____ 9. Bad or offensive

_____ 10. To find out

_____ 11. To bring distress or suffering to; plague

_____ 12. Obstructed

_____ 13. Inspired; captivated

_____ 14. Cloudy, misty, or hazy

_____ 15. Pale; dull

_____ 16. Withered; dry

_____ 17. Bruised

_____ 18. Enormous

_____ 19. Scoffing; ridicule

_____ 20. Can't be turned back

Poe Stories Vocabulary Fill In The Blanks 4 Answer Key

EPOCH	1. Age; time
CULPABLE	2. Responsible; at fault
APPARITION	3. A ghostly figure
SUCCUMBED	4. Gave in
COVETED	5. Wished for longingly
MANIFOLD	6. One of may kinds
CONCEIVED	7. To form or develop in the mind; devise
ECSTATIC	8. Euphoric; blissful
EGREGIOUS	9. Bad or offensive
ASCERTAIN	10. To find out
VEXED	11. To bring distress or suffering to; plague
IMPEDED	12. Obstructed
ENAMORED	13. Inspired; captivated
NEBULOUS	14. Cloudy, misty, or hazy
PALLID	15. Pale; dull
SERE	16. Withered; dry
LIVID	17. Bruised
PRODIGIOUS	18. Enormous
DERISION	19. Scoffing; ridicule
IRREVOCABLE	20. Can't be turned back

Poe Stories Vocabulary Matching 1

___ 1. DERISION
___ 2. SUCCUMBED
___ 3. ASUNDER
___ 4. VORACITY
___ 5. ENAMORED
___ 6. PERVERSENESS
___ 7. MANIFOLD
___ 8. SAGACIOUS
___ 9. EGREGIOUS
___ 10. CULPABLE
___ 11. COGNIZANT
___ 12. IRREVOCABLE
___ 13. EPOCH
___ 14. SAGACITY
___ 15. VEXED
___ 16. IMPUNITY
___ 17. NEBULOUS
___ 18. DISSIMULATION
___ 19. CONCEIVED
___ 20. PRODIGIOUS
___ 21. SERE
___ 22. LUCID
___ 23. APPARITION
___ 24. AUDACITY
___ 25. COUNTENANCES

A. Quality of being directed away from what is right or good; an appalling action, situation or object
B. Wild hunger
C. Aware; familiar with
D. Gave in
E. Scoffing; ridicule
F. Enormous
G. Cloudy, misty, or hazy
H. Withered; dry
I. To form or develop in the mind; devise
J. A ghostly figure
K. Concealing one's true feelings or intentions
L. Into separate parts or pieces
M. Exemption from punishment, penalty, or harm
N. Can't be turned back
O. Easily understood; sane or rational
P. To bring distress or suffering to; plague
Q. The quality of being discerning, sound in judgement
R. Responsible; at fault
S. One of may kinds
T. Boldness; daring
U. Faces
V. Inspired; captivated
W. Wise
X. Bad or offensive
Y. Age; time

Poe Stories Vocabulary Matching 1 Answer Key

E - 1. DERISION	A.	Quality of being directed away from what is right or good; an appalling action, situation or object
D - 2. SUCCUMBED	B.	Wild hunger
L - 3. ASUNDER	C.	Aware; familiar with
B - 4. VORACITY	D.	Gave in
V - 5. ENAMORED	E.	Scoffing; ridicule
A - 6. PERVERSENESS	F.	Enormous
S - 7. MANIFOLD	G.	Cloudy, misty, or hazy
W - 8. SAGACIOUS	H.	Withered; dry
X - 9. EGREGIOUS	I.	To form or develop in the mind; devise
R - 10. CULPABLE	J.	A ghostly figure
C - 11. COGNIZANT	K.	Concealing one's true feelings or intentions
N - 12. IRREVOCABLE	L.	Into separate parts or pieces
Y - 13. EPOCH	M.	Exemption from punishment, penalty, or harm
Q - 14. SAGACITY	N.	Can't be turned back
P - 15. VEXED	O.	Easily understood; sane or rational
M - 16. IMPUNITY	P.	To bring distress or suffering to; plague
G - 17. NEBULOUS	Q.	The quality of being discerning, sound in judgement
K - 18. DISSIMULATION	R.	Responsible; at fault
I - 19. CONCEIVED	S.	One of may kinds
F - 20. PRODIGIOUS	T.	Boldness; daring
H - 21. SERE	U.	Faces
O - 22. LUCID	V.	Inspired; captivated
J - 23. APPARITION	W.	Wise
T - 24. AUDACITY	X.	Bad or offensive
U - 25. COUNTENANCES	Y.	Age; time

Poe Stories Vocabulary Matching 2

___ 1. COUNTENANCES   A. Withered; dry
___ 2. MALEVOLENCE   B. One of may kinds
___ 3. MANIFOLD   C. Bruised
___ 4. PROMISCUOUSLY   D. Deceiving; diverting
___ 5. CONCEIVED   E. A hymn, composition, or service for the dead
___ 6. AUDACITY   F. Scoffing; ridicule
___ 7. DISSIMULATION   G. Boldness; daring
___ 8. ANNIHILATE   H. To reduce to nonexistence; to nullify or render void; abolish
___ 9. PRODIGIOUS   I. Ill will toward other; rancor; malice; evil influence, especially supernatural
___ 10. IMPEDED   J. Sensualness; voluptuousness
___ 11. EGRESS   K. Unnoticed
___ 12. ASUNDER   L. Inspired; captivated
___ 13. ORBS   M. Faces
___ 14. BEGUILING   N. To form or develop in the mind; devise
___ 15. MIEN   O. Causally; randomly
___ 16. LIVID   P. Into separate parts or pieces
___ 17. ENAMORED   Q. Responsible; at fault
___ 18. SULTRINESS   R. Wise
___ 19. REQUIEM   S. Concealing one's true feelings or intentions
___ 20. CULPABLE   T. Manner
___ 21. UNPERCEIVED   U. To strengthen or support with other evidence
___ 22. SAGACIOUS   V. Obstructed
___ 23. CORROBORATES   W. Enormous
___ 24. SERE   X. Exit; escape
___ 25. DERISION   Y. Eyes

Poe Stories Vocabulary Matching 2 Answer Key

M - 1. COUNTENANCES
I - 2. MALEVOLENCE
B - 3. MANIFOLD
O - 4. PROMISCUOUSLY
N - 5. CONCEIVED
G - 6. AUDACITY
S - 7. DISSIMULATION
H - 8. ANNIHILATE
W - 9. PRODIGIOUS
V - 10. IMPEDED
X - 11. EGRESS
P - 12. ASUNDER
Y - 13. ORBS
D - 14. BEGUILING
T - 15. MIEN
C - 16. LIVID
L - 17. ENAMORED
J - 18. SULTRINESS
E - 19. REQUIEM
Q - 20. CULPABLE
K - 21. UNPERCEIVED
R - 22. SAGACIOUS
U - 23. CORROBORATES
A - 24. SERE
F - 25. DERISION

A. Withered; dry
B. One of may kinds
C. Bruised
D. Deceiving; diverting
E. A hymn, composition, or service for the dead
F. Scoffing; ridicule
G. Boldness; daring
H. To reduce to nonexistence; to nullify or render void; abolish
I. Ill will toward other; rancor; malice; evil influence, especially supernatural
J. Sensualness; voluptuousness
K. Unnoticed
L. Inspired; captivated
M. Faces
N. To form or develop in the mind; devise
O. Causally; randomly
P. Into separate parts or pieces
Q. Responsible; at fault
R. Wise
S. Concealing one's true feelings or intentions
T. Manner
U. To strengthen or support with other evidence
V. Obstructed
W. Enormous
X. Exit; escape
Y. Eyes

Poe Stories Vocabulary Matching 3

___ 1. PALLID
___ 2. PRODIGIOUS
___ 3. AUDACITY
___ 4. MANIFOLD
___ 5. ENAMORED
___ 6. REQUIEM
___ 7. SUCCUMBED
___ 8. PERVERSENESS
___ 9. ECSTATIC
___ 10. SAGACIOUS
___ 11. ORBS
___ 12. COUNTENANCES
___ 13. EGREGIOUS
___ 14. CONSIGNED
___ 15. AMID
___ 16. ASCERTAIN
___ 17. LUCID
___ 18. SERE
___ 19. ODIOUS
___ 20. UNPERCEIVED
___ 21. COGNIZANT
___ 22. VEXED
___ 23. CULPABLE
___ 24. SUBLIME
___ 25. ASUNDER

A. Euphoric; blissful
B. Easily understood; sane or rational
C. Handed over
D. Eyes
E. To bring distress or suffering to; plague
F. Aware; familiar with
G. Quality of being directed away from what is right or good; an appalling action, situation or object
H. Into separate parts or pieces
I. A hymn, composition, or service for the dead
J. Withered; dry
K. To find out
L. Unnoticed
M. Bad or offensive
N. Enormous
O. Faces
P. Responsible; at fault
Q. Inspired; captivated
R. Boldness; daring
S. Pale; dull
T. Wise
U. Evoking feelings of repulsion
V. Gave in
W. One of may kinds
X. Majestic; inspiring awe; impressive
Y. In the middle of

Poe Stories Vocabulary Matching 3 Answer Key

S - 1.	PALLID	A. Euphoric; blissful
N - 2.	PRODIGIOUS	B. Easily understood; sane or rational
R - 3.	AUDACITY	C. Handed over
W - 4.	MANIFOLD	D. Eyes
Q - 5.	ENAMORED	E. To bring distress or suffering to; plague
I - 6.	REQUIEM	F. Aware; familiar with
V - 7.	SUCCUMBED	G. Quality of being directed away from what is right or good; an appalling action, situation or object
G - 8.	PERVERSENESS	H. Into separate parts or pieces
A - 9.	ECSTATIC	I. A hymn, composition, or service for the dead
T - 10.	SAGACIOUS	J. Withered; dry
D - 11.	ORBS	K. To find out
O - 12.	COUNTENANCES	L. Unnoticed
M - 13.	EGREGIOUS	M. Bad or offensive
C - 14.	CONSIGNED	N. Enormous
Y - 15.	AMID	O. Faces
K - 16.	ASCERTAIN	P. Responsible; at fault
B - 17.	LUCID	Q. Inspired; captivated
J - 18.	SERE	R. Boldness; daring
U - 19.	ODIOUS	S. Pale; dull
L - 20.	UNPERCEIVED	T. Wise
F - 21.	COGNIZANT	U. Evoking feelings of repulsion
E - 22.	VEXED	V. Gave in
P - 23.	CULPABLE	W. One of may kinds
X - 24.	SUBLIME	X. Majestic; inspiring awe; impressive
H - 25.	ASUNDER	Y. In the middle of

Poe Stories Vocabulary Matching 4

___ 1. NEBULOUS A. Obstructed
___ 2. IMPEDED B. To form or develop in the mind; devise
___ 3. REQUIEM C. A ghostly figure
___ 4. ECSTATIC D. Cloudy, misty, or hazy
___ 5. ASCERTAIN E. Into separate parts or pieces
___ 6. PERVERSENESS F. Exemption from punishment, penalty, or harm
___ 7. IMPUNITY G. Handed over
___ 8. COGNIZANT H. Sensualness; voluptuousness
___ 9. DISSIMULATION I. Gave in
___10. MANIFOLD J. Euphoric; blissful
___11. VEXED K. In the middle of
___12. SERE L. One of may kinds
___13. AUDACITY M. Withered; dry
___14. APPARITION N. Responsible; at fault
___15. CONCEIVED O. A hymn, composition, or service for the dead
___16. AMID P. Wild hunger
___17. SUCCUMBED Q. To bring distress or suffering to; plague
___18. CULPABLE R. Quality of being directed away from what is right or good; an appalling action, situation or object
___19. SULTRINESS S. Concealing one's true feelings or intentions
___20. CONSIGNED T. Aware; familiar with
___21. COVETED U. To find out
___22. LIVID V. Bruised
___23. VORACITY W. Boldness; daring
___24. UNPERCEIVED X. Unnoticed
___25. ASUNDER Y. Wished for longingly

Poe Stories Vocabulary Matching 4 Answer Key

D - 1.	NEBULOUS	A. Obstructed
A - 2.	IMPEDED	B. To form or develop in the mind; devise
O - 3.	REQUIEM	C. A ghostly figure
J - 4.	ECSTATIC	D. Cloudy, misty, or hazy
U - 5.	ASCERTAIN	E. Into separate parts or pieces
R - 6.	PERVERSENESS	F. Exemption from punishment, penalty, or harm
F - 7.	IMPUNITY	G. Handed over
T - 8.	COGNIZANT	H. Sensualness; voluptuousness
S - 9.	DISSIMULATION	I. Gave in
L - 10.	MANIFOLD	J. Euphoric; blissful
Q - 11.	VEXED	K. In the middle of
M - 12.	SERE	L. One of may kinds
W - 13.	AUDACITY	M. Withered; dry
C - 14.	APPARITION	N. Responsible; at fault
B - 15.	CONCEIVED	O. A hymn, composition, or service for the dead
K - 16.	AMID	P. Wild hunger
I - 17.	SUCCUMBED	Q. To bring distress or suffering to; plague
N - 18.	CULPABLE	R. Quality of being directed away from what is right or good; an appalling action, situation or object
H - 19.	SULTRINESS	S. Concealing one's true feelings or intentions
G - 20.	CONSIGNED	T. Aware; familiar with
Y - 21.	COVETED	U. To find out
V - 22.	LIVID	V. Bruised
P - 23.	VORACITY	W. Boldness; daring
X - 24.	UNPERCEIVED	X. Unnoticed
E - 25.	ASUNDER	Y. Wished for longingly

Poe Stories Vocabulary Magic Squares 1

Match the definition with the vocabulary word. Put your answers in the magic squares below. When your answers are correct, all columns and rows will add to the same number.

A. SAGACITY
B. CORROBORATES
C. CONCEIVED
D. IRREVOCABLE
E. AUDACITY
F. COGNIZANT
G. VEXED
H. UNPERCEIVED
I. DISSIMULATION
J. NEBULOUS
K. CULPABLE
L. REQUIEM
M. SUBLIME
N. VORACITY
O. COUNTENANCES
P. BEGUILING

1. Faces
2. Can't be turned back
3. Cloudy, misty, or hazy
4. Boldness; daring
5. Concealing one's true feelings or intentions
6. Aware; familiar with
7. Deceiving; diverting
8. To form or develop in the mind; devise
9. Unnoticed
10. Responsible; at fault
11. The quality of being discerning, sound in judgement
12. Wild hunger
13. To strengthen or support with other evidence
14. Majestic; inspiring awe; impressive
15. To bring distress or suffering to; plague
16. A hymn, composition, or service for the dead

A=	B=	C=	D=
E=	F=	G=	H=
I=	J=	K=	L=
M=	N=	O=	P=

Poe Stories Vocabulary Magic Squares 1 Answer Key

Match the definition with the vocabulary word. Put your answers in the magic squares below. When your answers are correct, all columns and rows will add to the same number.

A. SAGACITY
B. CORROBORATES
C. CONCEIVED
D. IRREVOCABLE
E. AUDACITY
F. COGNIZANT
G. VEXED
H. UNPERCEIVED
I. DISSIMULATION
J. NEBULOUS
K. CULPABLE
L. REQUIEM
M. SUBLIME
N. VORACITY
O. COUNTENANCES
P. BEGUILING

1. Faces
2. Can't be turned back
3. Cloudy, misty, or hazy
4. Boldness; daring
5. Concealing one's true feelings or intentions
6. Aware; familiar with
7. Deceiving; diverting
8. To form or develop in the mind; devise
9. Unnoticed
10. Responsible; at fault
11. The quality of being discerning, sound in judgement
12. Wild hunger
13. To strengthen or support with other evidence
14. Majestic; inspiring awe; impressive
15. To bring distress or suffering to; plague
16. A hymn, composition, or service for the dead

A=11	B=13	C=8	D=2
E=4	F=6	G=15	H=9
I=5	J=3	K=10	L=16
M=14	N=12	O=1	P=7

Poe Stories Vocabulary Magic Squares 2

Match the definition with the vocabulary word. Put your answers in the magic squares below. When your answers are correct, all columns and rows will add to the same number.

A. MANIFOLD
B. ODIOUS
C. IMPUNITY
D. ANNIHILATE
E. PROMISCUOUSLY
F. SULTRINESS
G. SAGACIOUS
H. SUBLIME
I. EGRESS
J. ASUNDER
K. VORACITY
L. ASTUTE
M. COUNTENANCES
N. ECSTATIC
O. COVETED
P. DERISION

1. One of may kinds
2. Euphoric; blissful
3. Into separate parts or pieces
4. Causally; randomly
5. Wise
6. Shrewd
7. Scoffing; ridicule
8. Exemption from punishment, penalty, or harm
9. Wished for longingly
10. To reduce to nonexistence; to nullify or render void; abolish
11. Majestic; inspiring awe; impressive
12. Wild hunger
13. Exit; escape
14. Sensualness; voluptuousness
15. Evoking feelings of repulsion
16. Faces

A=	B=	C=	D=
E=	F=	G=	H=
I=	J=	K=	L=
M=	N=	O=	P=

Poe Stories Vocabulary Magic Squares 2 Answer Key

Match the definition with the vocabulary word. Put your answers in the magic squares below. When your answers are correct, all columns and rows will add to the same number.

A. MANIFOLD
B. ODIOUS
C. IMPUNITY
D. ANNIHILATE
E. PROMISCUOUSLY
F. SULTRINESS
G. SAGACIOUS
H. SUBLIME
I. EGRESS
J. ASUNDER
K. VORACITY
L. ASTUTE
M. COUNTENANCES
N. ECSTATIC
O. COVETED
P. DERISION

1. One of may kinds
2. Euphoric; blissful
3. Into separate parts or pieces
4. Causally; randomly
5. Wise
6. Shrewd
7. Scoffing; ridicule
8. Exemption from punishment, penalty, or harm
9. Wished for longingly
10. To reduce to nonexistence; to nullify or render void; abolish
11. Majestic; inspiring awe; impressive
12. Wild hunger
13. Exit; escape
14. Sensualness; voluptuousness
15. Evoking feelings of repulsion
16. Faces

A=1	B=15	C=8	D=10
E=4	F=14	G=5	H=11
I=13	J=3	K=12	L=6
M=16	N=2	O=9	P=7

Poe Stories Vocabulary Magic Squares 3

Match the definition with the vocabulary word. Put your answers in the magic squares below. When your answers are correct, all columns and rows will add to the same number.

A. REQUIEM
B. SULTRINESS
C. ASUNDER
D. VEXED
E. ANNIHILATE
F. PROMISCUOUSLY
G. CULPABLE
H. CONCEIVED
I. EPOCH
J. DISSIMULATION
K. SAGACITY
L. APPARITION
M. MANIFOLD
N. AUDACITY
O. UNPERCEIVED
P. LUCID

1. Unnoticed
2. Concealing one's true feelings or intentions
3. To form or develop in the mind; devise
4. A hymn, composition, or service for the dead
5. To bring distress or suffering to; plague
6. To reduce to nonexistence; to nullify or render void; abolish
7. The quality of being discerning, sound in judgement
8. Boldness; daring
9. Causally; randomly
10. Into separate parts or pieces
11. One of may kinds
12. A ghostly figure
13. Age; time
14. Easily understood; sane or rational
15. Sensualness; voluptuousness
16. Responsible; at fault

A=	B=	C=	D=
E=	F=	G=	H=
I=	J=	K=	L=
M=	N=	O=	P=

Poe Stories Vocabulary Magic Squares 3 Answer Key

Match the definition with the vocabulary word. Put your answers in the magic squares below. When your answers are correct, all columns and rows will add to the same number.

A. REQUIEM
B. SULTRINESS
C. ASUNDER
D. VEXED
E. ANNIHILATE
F. PROMISCUOUSLY
G. CULPABLE
H. CONCEIVED
I. EPOCH
J. DISSIMULATION
K. SAGACITY
L. APPARITION
M. MANIFOLD
N. AUDACITY
O. UNPERCEIVED
P. LUCID

1. Unnoticed
2. Concealing one's true feelings or intentions
3. To form or develop in the mind; devise
4. A hymn, composition, or service for the dead
5. To bring distress or suffering to; plague
6. To reduce to nonexistence; to nullify or render void; abolish
7. The quality of being discerning, sound in judgement
8. Boldness; daring
9. Causally; randomly
10. Into separate parts or pieces
11. One of may kinds
12. A ghostly figure
13. Age; time
14. Easily understood; sane or rational
15. Sensualness; voluptuousness
16. Responsible; at fault

A=4	B=15	C=10	D=5
E=6	F=9	G=16	H=3
I=13	J=2	K=7	L=12
M=11	N=8	O=1	P=14

Poe Stories Vocabulary Magic Squares 4

Match the definition with the vocabulary word. Put your answers in the magic squares below. When your answers are correct, all columns and rows will add to the same number.

A. DERISION
B. EPOCH
C. REQUIEM
D. AMID
E. COGNIZANT
F. BEGUILING
G. EGREGIOUS
H. IMPEDED
I. UNPERCEIVED
J. PERVERSENESS
K. ANNIHILATE
L. CORROBORATES
M. PRODIGIOUS
N. PALLID
O. ECSTATIC
P. CONCEIVED

1. Obstructed
2. Enormous
3. Age; time
4. To reduce to nonexistence; to nullify or render void; abolish
5. Quality of being directed away from what is right or good; an appalling action, situation or object
6. A hymn, composition, or service for the dead
7. To form or develop in the mind; devise
8. Aware; familiar with
9. Euphoric; blissful
10. Deceiving; diverting
11. Unnoticed
12. In the middle of
13. Scoffing; ridicule
14. To strengthen or support with other evidence
15. Bad or offensive
16. Pale; dull

A = 13	B = 3	C = 6	D = 12
E = 8	F = 10	G = 15	H = 1
I = 11	J = 5	K = 4	L = 14
M = 2	N = 16	O = 9	P = 7

Poe Stories Vocabulary Magic Squares 4 Answer Key

Match the definition with the vocabulary word. Put your answers in the magic squares below. When your answers are correct, all columns and rows will add to the same number.

A. DERISION
B. EPOCH
C. REQUIEM
D. AMID
E. COGNIZANT
F. BEGUILING
G. EGREGIOUS
H. IMPEDED
I. UNPERCEIVED
J. PERVERSENESS
K. ANNIHILATE
L. CORROBORATES
M. PRODIGIOUS
N. PALLID
O. ECSTATIC
P. CONCEIVED

1. Obstructed
2. Enormous
3. Age; time
4. To reduce to nonexistence; to nullify or render void; abolish
5. Quality of being directed away from what is right or good; an appalling action, situation or object
6. A hymn, composition, or service for the dead
7. To form or develop in the mind; devise
8. Aware; familiar with
9. Euphoric; blissful
10. Deceiving; diverting
11. Unnoticed
12. In the middle of
13. Scoffing; ridicule
14. To strengthen or support with other evidence
15. Bad or offensive
16. Pale; dull

A=13	B=3	C=6	D=12
E=8	F=10	G=15	H=1
I=11	J=5	K=4	L=14
M=2	N=16	O=9	P=7

Poe Stories Vocabulary Word Search 1

Words are placed backwards, forward, diagonally, up and down. Clues listed below can help you find the words. Circle the hidden vocabulary words in the maze.

```
A S T U T E R G S M M Q W L X V Q Y M
D S A G A C I O U S V A L D V O T W M
H T S F S X Y S L P K S N S D I V G S
N A S X U N U T T A U K U I C Y D B W
M P N L B O F J R O S O O A F E R W R
K Z N N L T G N I L I U G E B O D W C
H L E U I R G G N G S A N M G E L Q C
B I B G M H I B E V S C U D V R D D T
M E C N E D I R S V E C L I E I E R Q
N A C O O Z G L S H C X E P V R C S Y
O X P R U E P H A U C C E I O C N E S
I N P P B N R L S T R P L D R O E R K
S C L Z A C T M P E E R M D A N L E Q
I K U L L R X E P T M O I E C S O C Z
R J C L D F I N N M R M C D I I V O J
E P N I P K U T R A A I S E T G E V X
D N C E M A N K I E N S L P Y N L E W
B U A B C P B K L O Q C L M Y E A T G
L E P M K S U L B M N U E I Y D M E B
P P A S O R T N E Z F O I S X W L D T
B O L Q G R F A I F B U C E R H F G Y
Y C L S N K E P T T P S X H M Z F S W
S H I D G J B D M I Y L D P X S H H S
T V D E V I E C N O C Y T I C A D U A
```

A ghostly figure (10)
A hymn, composition, or service for the dead (7)
Age; time (5)
Bad or offensive (9)
Boldness; daring (8)
Bruised (5)
Causally; randomly (13)
Cloudy, misty, or hazy (8)
Deceiving; diverting (9)
Easily understood; sane or rational (5)
Enormous (10)
Euphoric; blissful (8)
Evoking feelings of repulsion (6)
Exemption from punishment, penalty, or harm (8)
Exit; escape (6)
Eyes (4)
Faces (12)
Gave in (9)
Handed over (9)
Ill will toward other; rancor; malice; evil influence, especially supernatural (11)
In the middle of (4)
Inspired; captivated (8)
Into separate parts or pieces (7)
Majestic; inspiring awe; impressive (7)
Manner (4)
Obstructed (7)
One of may kinds (8)
Pale; dull (6)
Responsible; at fault (8)
Scoffing; ridicule (8)
Sensualness; voluptuousness (10)
Shrewd (6)
The quality of being discerning, sound in judgement (8)
To bring distress or suffering to; plague (5)
To form or develop in the mind; devise (9)
To reduce to nonexistence; to nullify or render void; abolish (10)
Unnoticed (11)
Wild hunger (8)
Wise (9)
Wished for longingly (7)
Withered; dry (4)

Poe Stories Vocabulary Word Search 1 Answer Key

Words are placed backwards, forward, diagonally, up and down. Clues listed below can help you find the words. Circle the hidden vocabulary words in the maze.

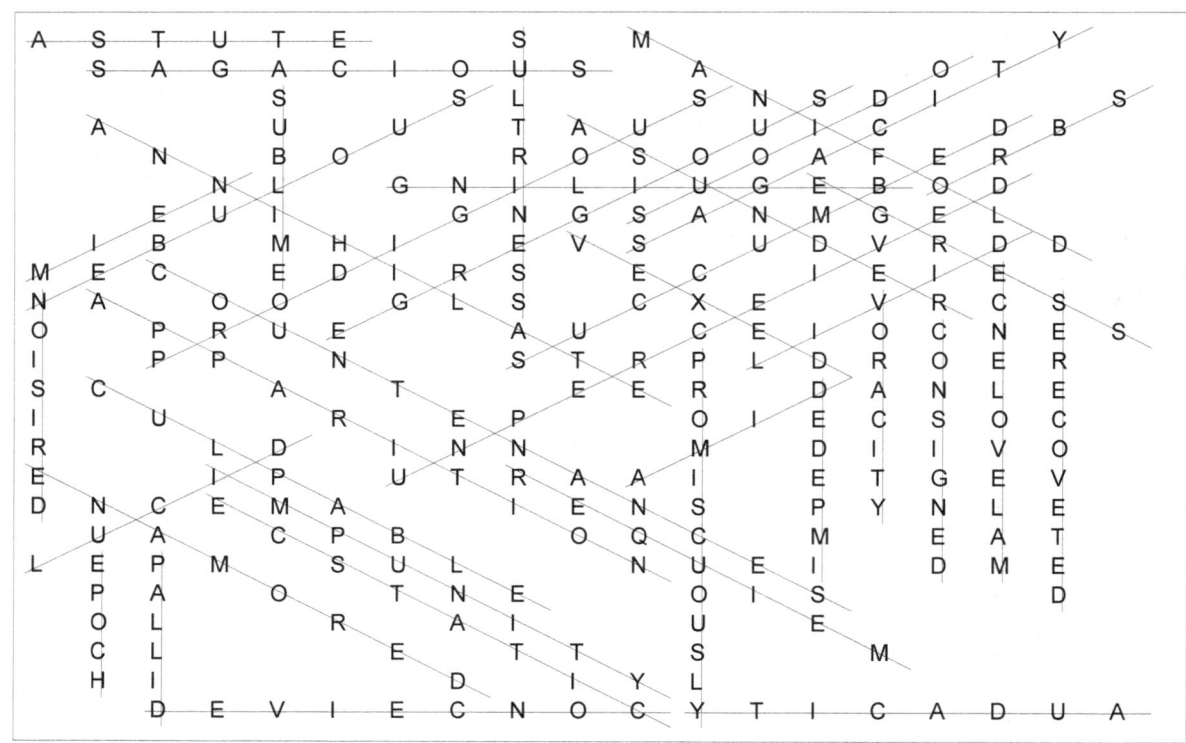

A ghostly figure (10)
A hymn, composition, or service for the dead (7)
Age; time (5)
Bad or offensive (9)
Boldness; daring (8)
Bruised (5)
Causally; randomly (13)
Cloudy, misty, or hazy (8)
Deceiving; diverting (9)
Easily understood; sane or rational (5)
Enormous (10)
Euphoric; blissful (8)
Evoking feelings of repulsion (6)
Exemption from punishment, penalty, or harm (8)
Exit; escape (6)
Eyes (4)
Faces (12)
Gave in (9)
Handed over (9)
Ill will toward other; rancor; malice; evil influence, especially supernatural (11)

In the middle of (4)
Inspired; captivated (8)
Into separate parts or pieces (7)
Majestic; inspiring awe; impressive (7)
Manner (4)
Obstructed (7)
One of may kinds (8)
Pale; dull (6)
Responsible; at fault (8)
Scoffing; ridicule (8)
Sensualness; voluptuousness (10)
Shrewd (6)
The quality of being discerning, sound in judgement (8)
To bring distress or suffering to; plague (5)
To form or develop in the mind; devise (9)
To reduce to nonexistence; to nullify or render void; abolish (10)
Unnoticed (11)
Wild hunger (8)
Wise (9)
Wished for longingly (7)
Withered; dry (4)

Poe Stories Vocabulary Word Search 2

Words are placed backwards, forward, diagonally, up and down. Clues listed below can help you find the words. Circle the hidden vocabulary words in the maze.

```
D Z G R S E T A R O B O R R O C T S N
E I M E U P R W N R E Q U I E M U U J
V V S C B T R X R N H B B C C L C C L
I V U S L S T O O D I O U S T Q O C H
E N O T I N A N D M G H W R N F N U G
C Y I A M M N G C I S W I Z E L C M M
R X G T E V U G A N G N K L X M E B Q
E S E I W C R L X C E I B J A J I E H
P W R C Z B Y Z A S I A O L F T V D K
N J G C F S F B S T C O W U K J E A W
U D E R O M A N E O I F U M S J D S L
B E Z H Q N J K V S N O K S M S K C C
M Z P F M Q S E S V Q Y N C N U P E V
V A S O D Y R I A V K T V X Q O X R S
K C N B C R K X G F V I V O S L X T D
G O I I I H M J A N S C B E R U F A R
A G M E F V B M C G E A X S X B D I L
S N P G N O I S I R E D I M A E S N G
T I U R P R L B T E P U C M T N D Y H
U Z N E A A W D Y D N A F E P H F G K
T A I S L C D N V N H Z V J M E H H W
E N T S L I V I D U Z O S E R E D S S
M T Y X I T Z C R S C K M G B D J E Y
L U C I D Y E L B A P L U C T S L X D
```

A hymn, composition, or service for the dead (7)
Age; time (5)
Aware; familiar with (9)
Bad or offensive (9)
Boldness; daring (8)
Bruised (5)
Can't be turned back (11)
Cloudy, misty, or hazy (8)
Concealing one's true feelings or intentions (13)
Easily understood; sane or rational (5)
Enormous (10)
Euphoric; blissful (8)
Evoking feelings of repulsion (6)
Exemption from punishment, penalty, or harm (8)
Exit; escape (6)
Eyes (4)
Gave in (9)
Handed over (9)
In the middle of (4)
Inspired; captivated (8)
Into separate parts or pieces (7)

Majestic; inspiring awe; impressive (7)
Manner (4)
Obstructed (7)
One of may kinds (8)
Pale; dull (6)
Responsible; at fault (8)
Scoffing; ridicule (8)
Sensualness; voluptuousness (10)
Shrewd (6)
The quality of being discerning, sound in judgement (8)
To bring distress or suffering to; plague (5)
To find out (9)
To form or develop in the mind; devise (9)
To reduce to nonexistence; to nullify or render void; abolish (10)
To strengthen or support with other evidence (12)
Unnoticed (11)
Wild hunger (8)
Wise (9)
Wished for longingly (7)
Withered; dry (4)

Poe Stories Vocabulary Word Search 2 Answer Key

Words are placed backwards, forward, diagonally, up and down. Clues listed below can help you find the words. Circle the hidden vocabulary words in the maze.

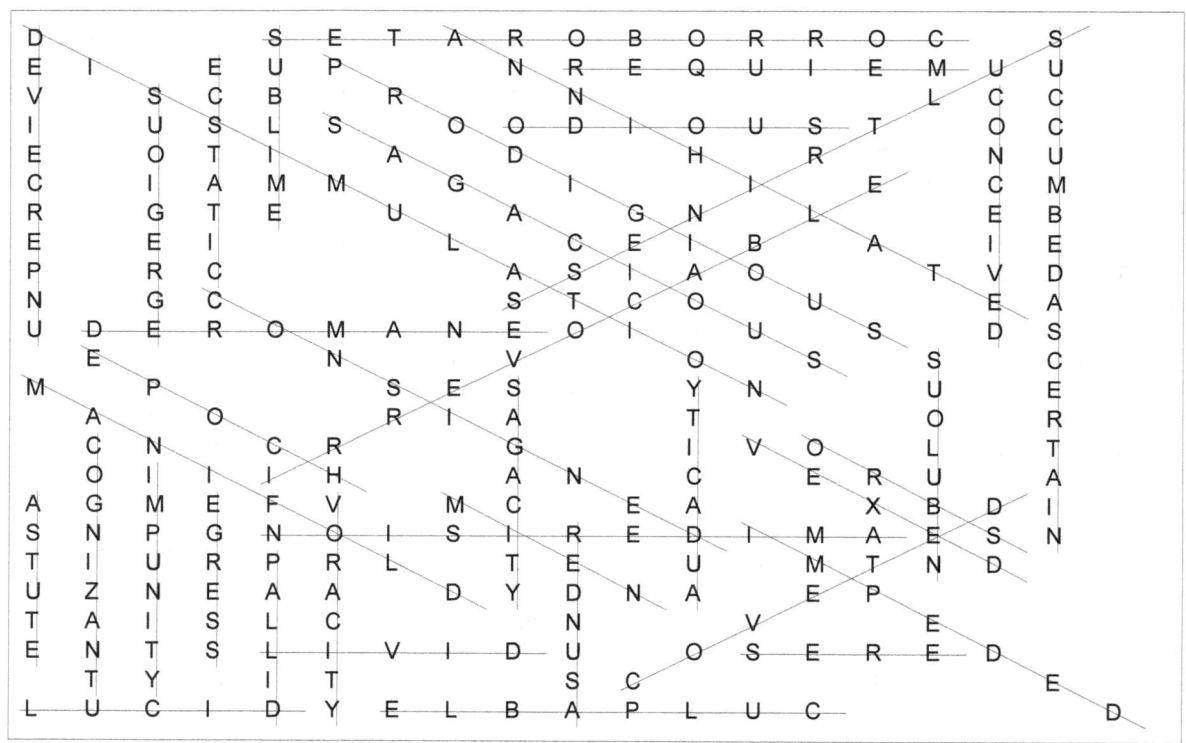

A hymn, composition, or service for the dead (7)
Age; time (5)
Aware; familiar with (9)
Bad or offensive (9)
Boldness; daring (8)
Bruised (5)
Can't be turned back (11)
Cloudy, misty, or hazy (8)
Concealing one's true feelings or intentions (13)
Easily understood; sane or rational (5)
Enormous (10)
Euphoric; blissful (8)
Evoking feelings of repulsion (6)
Exemption from punishment, penalty, or harm (8)
Exit; escape (6)
Eyes (4)
Gave in (9)
Handed over (9)
In the middle of (4)
Inspired; captivated (8)
Into separate parts or pieces (7)

Majestic; inspiring awe; impressive (7)
Manner (4)
Obstructed (7)
One of may kinds (8)
Pale; dull (6)
Responsible; at fault (8)
Scoffing; ridicule (8)
Sensualness; voluptuousness (10)
Shrewd (6)
The quality of being discerning, sound in judgement (8)
To bring distress or suffering to; plague (5)
To find out (9)
To form or develop in the mind; devise (9)
To reduce to nonexistence; to nullify or render void; abolish (10)
To strengthen or support with other evidence (12)
Unnoticed (11)
Wild hunger (8)
Wise (9)
Wished for longingly (7)
Withered; dry (4)

Poe Stories Vocabulary Word Search 3

Words are placed backwards, forward, diagonally, up and down. Words listed below are included in the maze. Circle the hidden vocabulary words in the maze.

```
A P P A R I T I O N S R I M P E D E D
C A N N I H I L A T E C L I M J Y E
O B C Z Q K Z L W B V Q O P R A L S V
N K U R N X B Y G P R U N S R L J U I
S Q L J J Q L R R M H I C K E E M L E
I X P P F Z V O Y M N E E D V A T C
G X A M X S D V T V X M I E O O N R R
N R B L T I L C I I Z K V R C L I E
E E L A G N U K C V M V E O A E F N P
D D E I M C C M A P O P D M B N O E N
S N O X V I I U G R X P U A L C L S U
V U Z P Z I D H A P M I E N E E D S C
S S C M R A D C S D P P G E I Q K U O
P A P C C O I Z K Z O X R C C T F O R
A D Q I U T M T R C Y H E S O B Y L R
L L T A Y M C I H T A S G T G E S U O
Y D S N W B O S V S E I A N G A B B
I V E C C X R E V C T R O T I U G E O
D F R E B B L C D E U E U I Z I A N R
G W I R S J T E G X T O S C A L C N A
Y R S T L C X R J F E E U D N I I P T
Q Y I A S E E K Z X P M D S T N O K E
R H O I V S C O D I O U S X L G U X S
R K N N S U B L I M E S K G J Y S P Z
```

AMID	ECSTATIC	ORBS
ANNIHILATE	EGREGIOUS	PALLID
APPARITION	EGRESS	PRODIGIOUS
ASCERTAIN	ENAMORED	PROMISCUOUSLY
ASTUTE	EPOCH	REQUIEM
ASUNDER	IMPEDED	SAGACIOUS
AUDACITY	IMPUNITY	SAGACITY
BEGUILING	IRREVOCABLE	SERE
COGNIZANT	LIVID	SUBLIME
CONCEIVED	LUCID	SUCCUMBED
CONSIGNED	MALEVOLENCE	SULTRINESS
CORROBORATES	MANIFOLD	UNPERCEIVED
COVETED	MIEN	VEXED
CULPABLE	NEBULOUS	VORACITY
DERISION	ODIOUS	

Poe Stories Vocabulary Word Search 3 Answer Key

Words are placed backwards, forward, diagonally, up and down. Words listed below are included in the maze. Circle the hidden vocabulary words in the maze.

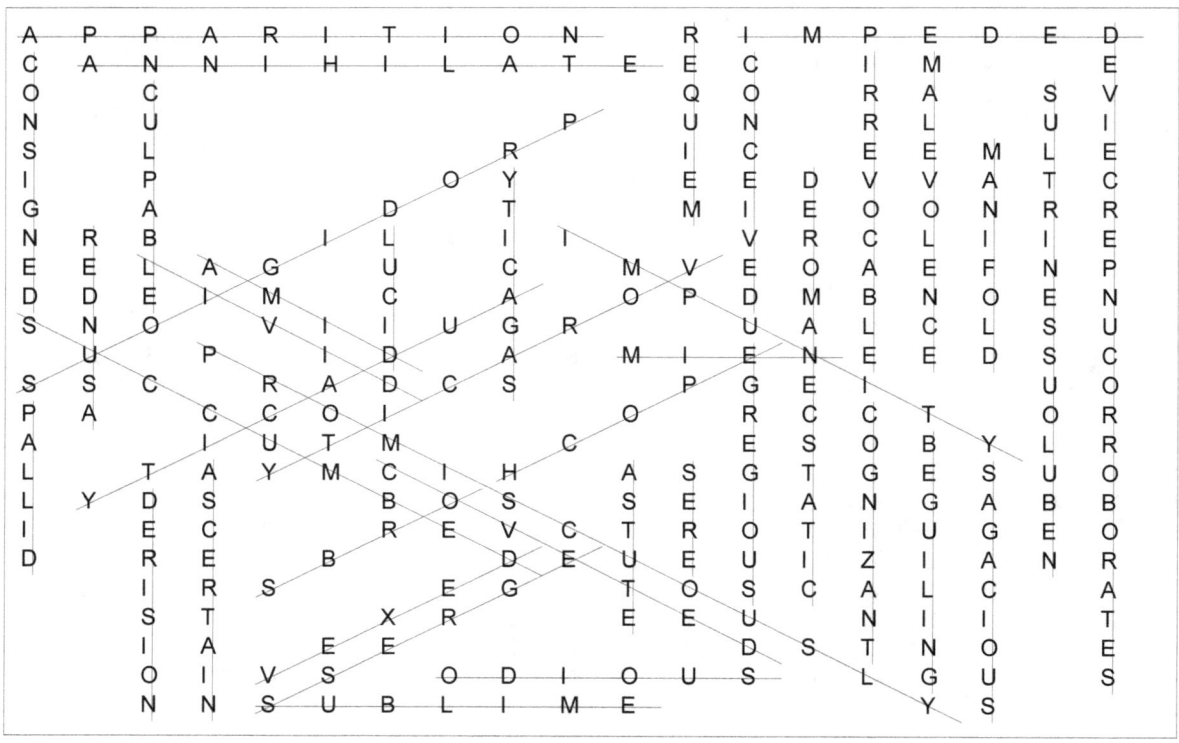

AMID	ECSTATIC	ORBS
ANNIHILATE	EGREGIOUS	PALLID
APPARITION	EGRESS	PRODIGIOUS
ASCERTAIN	ENAMORED	PROMISCUOUSLY
ASTUTE	EPOCH	REQUIEM
ASUNDER	IMPEDED	SAGACIOUS
AUDACITY	IMPUNITY	SAGACITY
BEGUILING	IRREVOCABLE	SERE
COGNIZANT	LIVID	SUBLIME
CONCEIVED	LUCID	SUCCUMBED
CONSIGNED	MALEVOLENCE	SULTRINESS
CORROBORATES	MANIFOLD	UNPERCEIVED
COVETED	MIEN	VEXED
CULPABLE	NEBULOUS	VORACITY
DERISION	ODIOUS	

Poe Stories Vocabulary Word Search 4

Words are placed backwards, forward, diagonally, up and down. Words listed below are included in the maze. Circle the hidden vocabulary words in the maze.

```
C O V E T E D E R I S I O N N Y C D M
W O Q S P L W E N L F M E H T O I I F
F X N R J O Q G B I J I Y I N C T M W
Z W T S Z U C L F V M G C C U M A A L
P A L L I D V H D I Z A E L S S T X V
C V U E E G T N Z D G I Z U U E S C P
O R M D T S N L S A V H O B O N C C W
U X D H A U J E S E R I L C I A E H D
N Z I V L C J Y D R C I G E G M R Z J
T F S X I C I J Q A M W N G I O F V W
E Q S N H U J T G E M H I R D R F L L
N D I V I M X A Y B A T L E O E W S V
A P M O N B S I N B L J I G R D U B V
N E U R N E L M T H E V U I P O S J P
C R L A A D T P X N V M G O L Q A W Z
E V A C S V N U T O O M E U C X S P P
S E T I G T V N V I L Z B S O D C S N
P R I T G B U I M T E E S K G L E Y N
V S O Y S U L T R I N E S S N O R B S
K E N L U H J Y E R C F E S I F T S J
R N X T O H N P Z A E X R T Z I A E K
T E M E I X S L L P J Q G Y A N I R P
A S U N D E R I M P E D E D N A N E H
Z S K M O C U L P A B L E S T M W F D
```

AMID	DISSIMULATION	ORBS
ANNIHILATE	ECSTATIC	PALLID
APPARITION	EGREGIOUS	PERVERSENESS
ASCERTAIN	EGRESS	PRODIGIOUS
ASTUTE	ENAMORED	REQUIEM
ASUNDER	EPOCH	SAGACIOUS
AUDACITY	IMPEDED	SAGACITY
BEGUILING	IMPUNITY	SERE
COGNIZANT	LIVID	SUBLIME
CONCEIVED	LUCID	SUCCUMBED
CONSIGNED	MALEVOLENCE	SULTRINESS
COUNTENANCES	MANIFOLD	VEXED
COVETED	MIEN	VORACITY
CULPABLE	NEBULOUS	
DERISION	ODIOUS	

Poe Stories Vocabulary Word Search 4 Answer Key

Words are placed backwards, forward, diagonally, up and down. Words listed below are included in the maze. Circle the hidden vocabulary words in the maze.

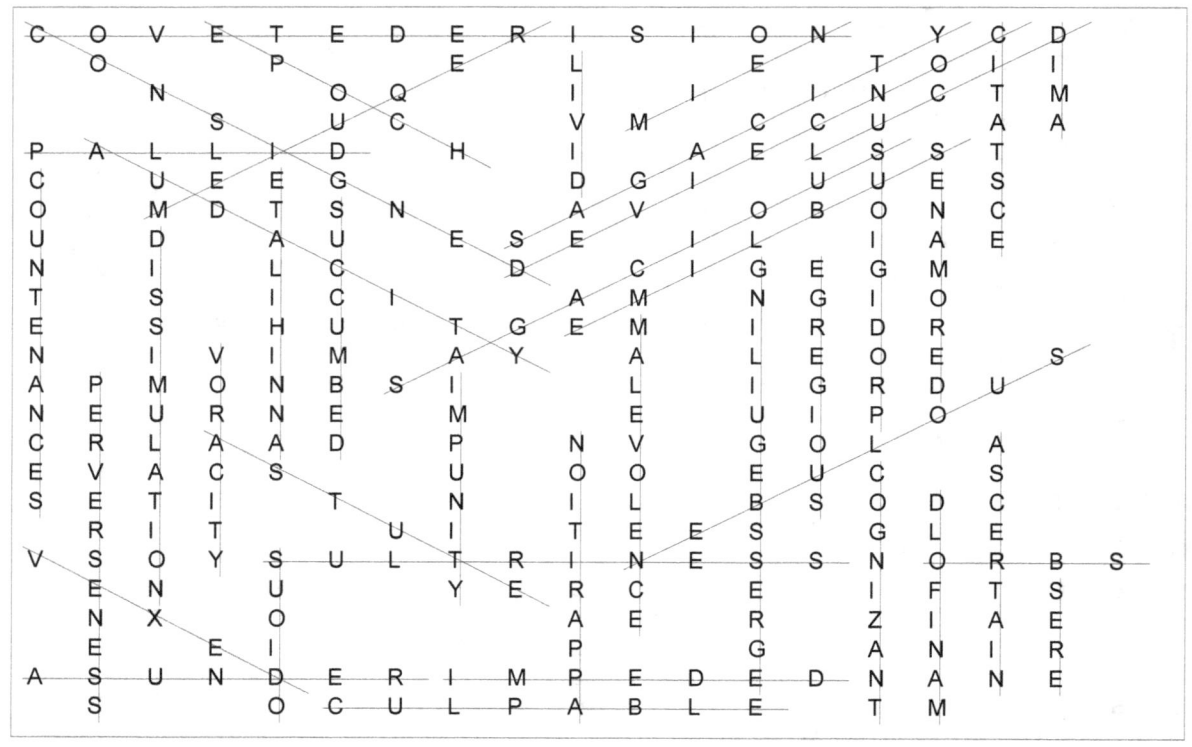

AMID	DISSIMULATION	ORBS
ANNIHILATE	ECSTATIC	PALLID
APPARITION	EGREGIOUS	PERVERSENESS
ASCERTAIN	EGRESS	PRODIGIOUS
ASTUTE	ENAMORED	REQUIEM
ASUNDER	EPOCH	SAGACIOUS
AUDACITY	IMPEDED	SAGACITY
BEGUILING	IMPUNITY	SERE
COGNIZANT	LIVID	SUBLIME
CONCEIVED	LUCID	SUCCUMBED
CONSIGNED	MALEVOLENCE	SULTRINESS
COUNTENANCES	MANIFOLD	VEXED
COVETED	MIEN	VORACITY
CULPABLE	NEBULOUS	
DERISION	ODIOUS	

Poe Stories Vocabulary Crossword 1

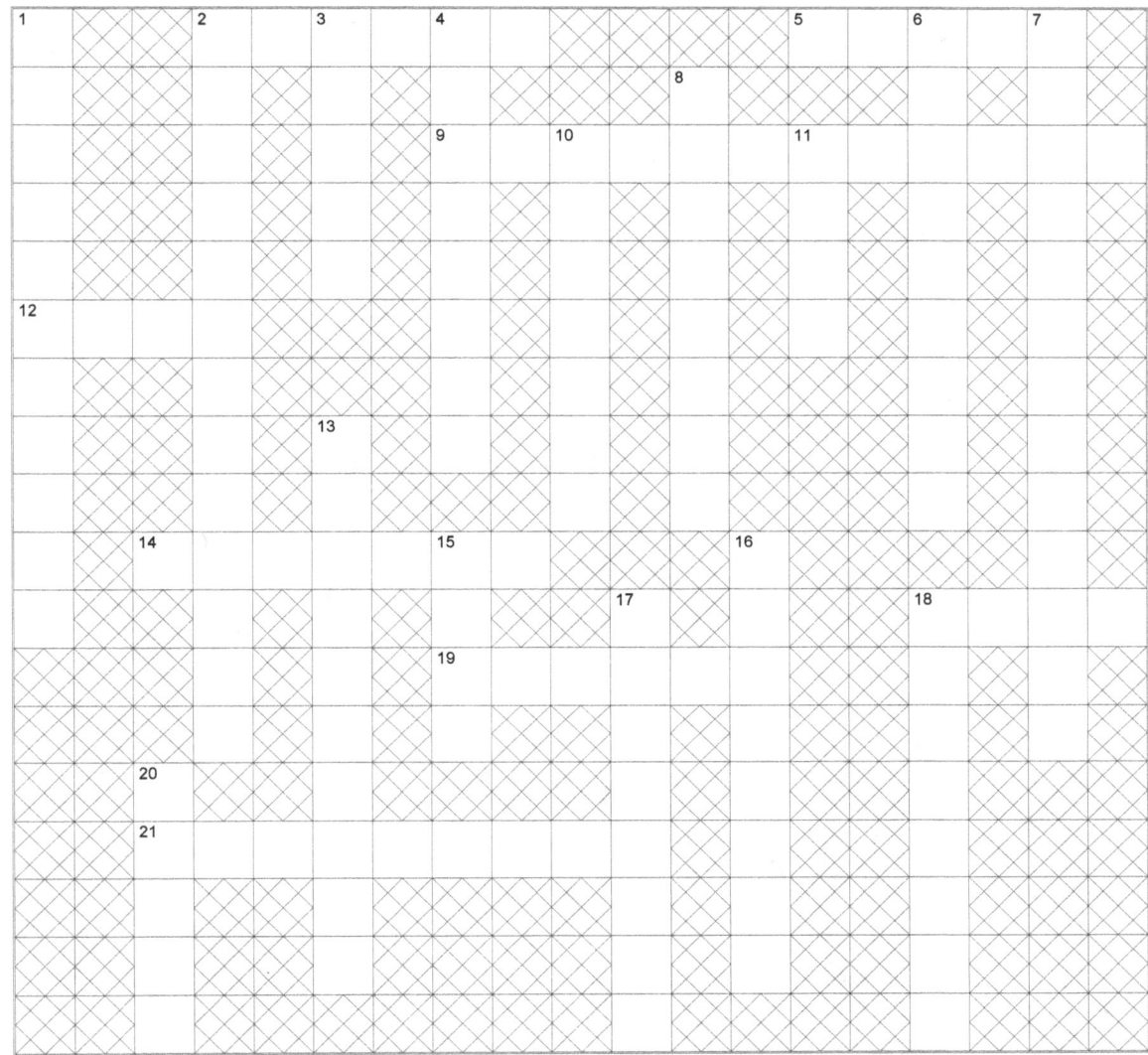

Across
2. Pale; dull
5. Easily understood; sane or rational
9. Quality of being directed away from what is right or good; an appalling action, situation or object
12. Eyes
14. Majestic; inspiring awe; impressive
18. In the middle of
19. Exit; escape
21. Bad or offensive

Down
1. Ill will toward other; rancor; malice; evil influence, especially supernatural
2. Causally; randomly
3. Bruised
4. Exemption from punishment, penalty, or harm
6. To form or develop in the mind; devise
7. Concealing one's true feelings or intentions
8. Cloudy, misty, or hazy
10. A hymn, composition, or service for the dead
11. Withered; dry
13. Sensualness; voluptuousness
15. Manner
16. Euphoric; blissful
17. Scoffing; ridicule
18. Boldness; daring
20. To bring distress or suffering to; plague

Poe Stories Vocabulary Crossword 1 Answer Key

	1 M		2 P	A	3 L	L	4 I	D			5 L	U	6 C	I	7 D
	A		R		I		M			8 N			O		I
	L		O	V		9 P	10 E	R	V	E	R	11 S	E	N	E	S	S

(Puzzle grid — answer key)

Across
2. Pale; dull — PALLID
5. Easily understood; sane or rational — LUCID
9. Quality of being directed away from what is right or good; an appalling action, situation or object — PERVERSENESS
12. Eyes — ORBS
14. Majestic; inspiring awe; impressive — SUBLIME
18. In the middle of — AMID
19. Exit; escape — EGRESS
21. Bad or offensive — EGREGIOUS

Down
1. Ill will toward other; rancor; malice; evil influence, especially supernatural — MALEVOLENCE
2. Causally; randomly — PROMISCUOUSLY
3. Bruised — LIVID
4. Exemption from punishment, penalty, or harm — IMPUNITY
6. To form or develop in the mind; devise — CONCEIVE
7. Concealing one's true feelings or intentions — DISSIMULATION
8. Cloudy, misty, or hazy — NEBULOUS
10. A hymn, composition, or service for the dead — REQUIEM
11. Withered; dry — SEARED
13. Sensualness; voluptuousness — SYBARITISM
15. Manner — MIEN
16. Euphoric; blissful — ECSTATIC
17. Scoffing; ridicule — DERISION
18. Boldness; daring — AUDACITY
20. To bring distress or suffering to; plague — VEX

Poe Stories Vocabulary Crossword 2

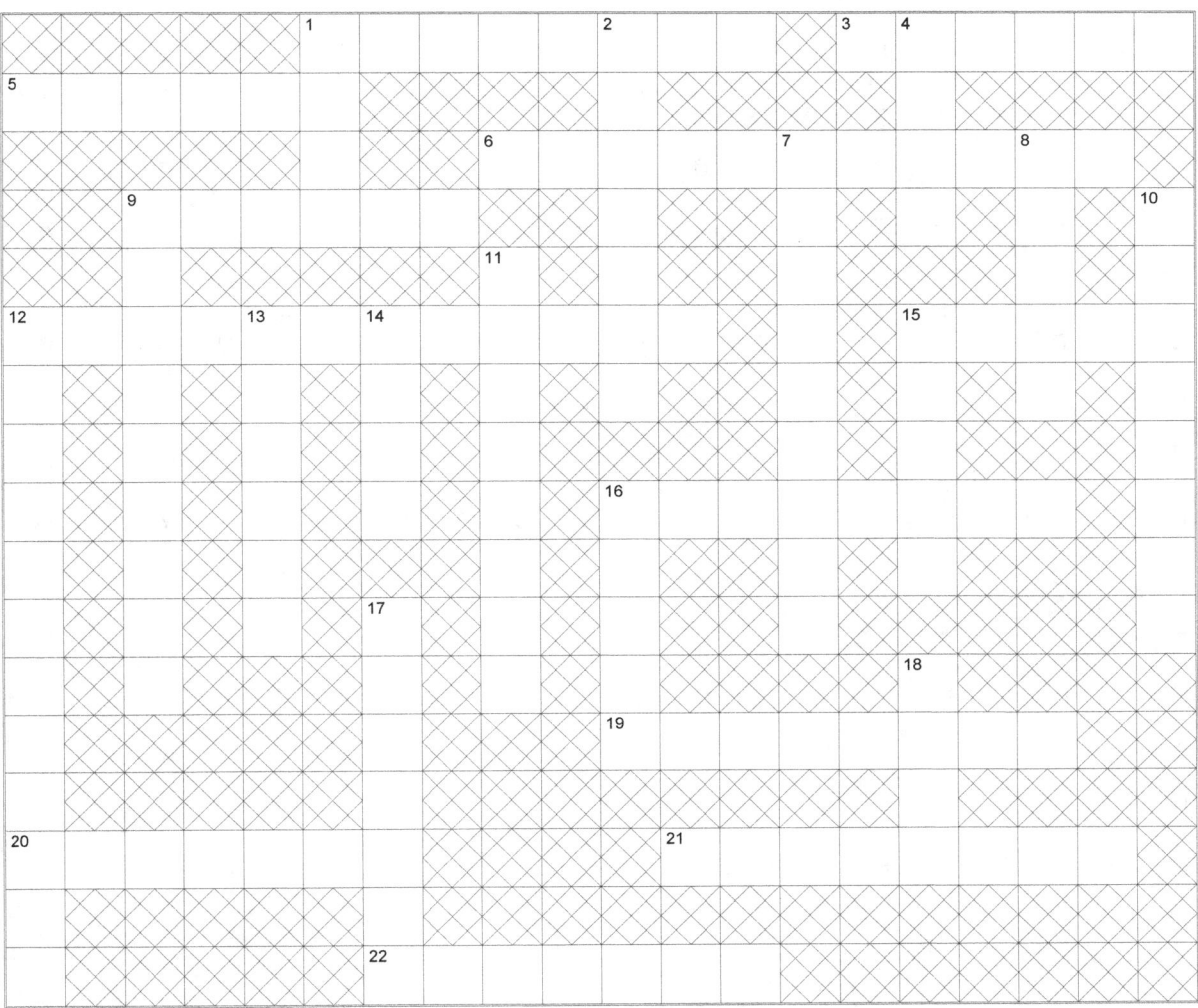

Across
1. The quality of being discerning, sound in judgement
3. Pale; dull
5. Shrewd
6. Unnoticed
9. Exit; escape
12. To strengthen or support with other evidence
15. Easily understood; sane or rational
16. Wild hunger
19. Scoffing; ridicule
20. Wished for longingly
21. Exemption from punishment, penalty, or harm
22. A hymn, composition, or service for the dead

Down
1. Withered; dry
2. Obstructed
4. In the middle of
7. Aware; familiar with
8. Age; time
9. Bad or offensive
10. Boldness; daring
11. One of may kinds
12. Faces
13. Evoking feelings of repulsion
14. Eyes
15. Bruised
16. To bring distress or suffering to; plague
17. Into separate parts or pieces
18. Manner

Poe Stories Vocabulary Crossword 2 Answer Key

					1 S	A	G	A	C	2 I	T	Y		3 P	4 A	L	L	I	D
5 A	S	T	U	T	E					M					M				
					R		6 U	N	P	E	R	7 C	E	I	V	8 E	D		
		9 E	G	R	E	S	S			E		O			D		P		10 A
		G					11 M	D				G					O		U
12 C	O	R	R	13 O	14 B	O	R	A	T	E	S			15 L	U	C	I	D	
O		E		D		R		N		D		I		I		H		A	
U		G		I		B		I				Z		V				C	
N		I		O		S		F		16 V	O	R	A	C	I	T	Y	I	
T		O		U				O		E		N		D				T	
E		U		S		17 A		L		X		T						Y	
N		S				S		D		E				18 M					
A				S		U				19 D	E	R	I	S	I	O	N		
N				U		N								E					
20 C	O	V	E	T	E	D				21 I	M	P	U	N	I	T	Y		
E						E													
S						22 R	E	Q	U	I	E	M							

Across
1. The quality of being discerning, sound in judgement
3. Pale; dull
5. Shrewd
6. Unnoticed
9. Exit; escape
12. To strengthen or support with other evidence
15. Easily understood; sane or rational
16. Wild hunger
19. Scoffing; ridicule
20. Wished for longingly
21. Exemption from punishment, penalty, or harm
22. A hymn, composition, or service for the dead

Down
1. Withered; dry
2. Obstructed
4. In the middle of
7. Aware; familiar with
8. Age; time
9. Bad or offensive
10. Boldness; daring
11. One of may kinds
12. Faces
13. Evoking feelings of repulsion
14. Eyes
15. Bruised
16. To bring distress or suffering to; plague
17. Into separate parts or pieces
18. Manner

Poe Stories Vocabulary Crossword 3

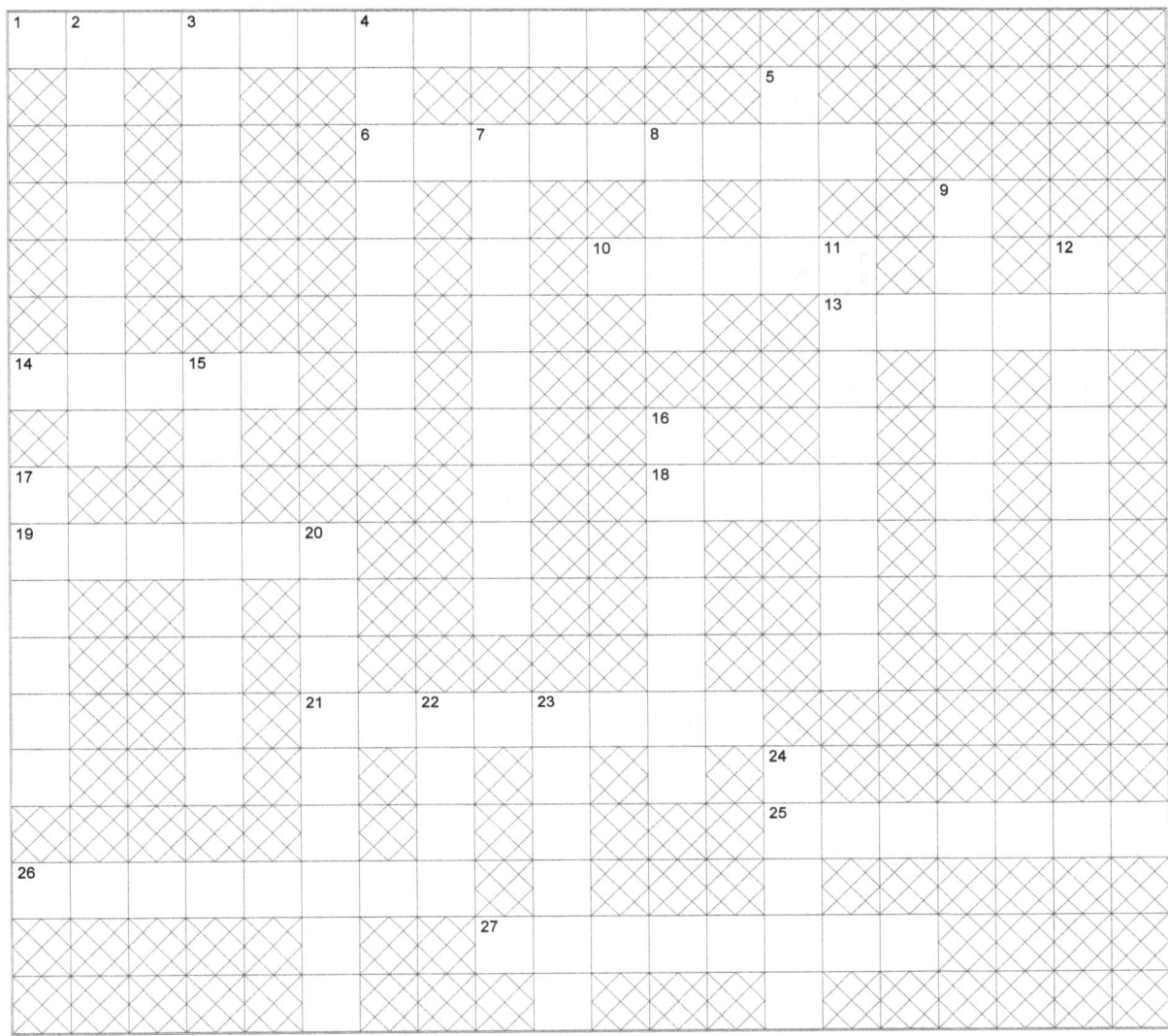

Across
1. Unnoticed
6. Gave in
10. To bring distress or suffering to; plague
13. Exit; escape
14. Easily understood; sane or rational
18. Eyes
19. Shrewd
21. Inspired; captivated
25. Obstructed
26. One of may kinds
27. Boldness; daring

Down
2. Cloudy, misty, or hazy
3. Age; time
4. Euphoric; blissful
5. Withered; dry
7. Handed over
8. Manner
9. Wild hunger
11. Scoffing; ridicule
12. Into separate parts or pieces
15. Exemption from punishment, penalty, or harm
16. Wished for longingly
17. Pale; dull
20. Bad or offensive
22. In the middle of
23. Evoking feelings of repulsion
24. Bruised

Poe Stories Vocabulary Crossword 3 Answer Key

Across
1. Unnoticed
6. Gave in
10. To bring distress or suffering to; plague
13. Exit; escape
14. Easily understood; sane or rational
18. Eyes
19. Shrewd
21. Inspired; captivated
25. Obstructed
26. One of may kinds
27. Boldness; daring

Down
2. Cloudy, misty, or hazy
3. Age; time
4. Euphoric; blissful
5. Withered; dry
7. Handed over
8. Manner
9. Wild hunger
11. Scoffing; ridicule
12. Into separate parts or pieces
15. Exemption from punishment, penalty, or harm
16. Wished for longingly
17. Pale; dull
20. Bad or offensive
22. In the middle of
23. Evoking feelings of repulsion
24. Bruised

Poe Stories Vocabulary Crossword 4

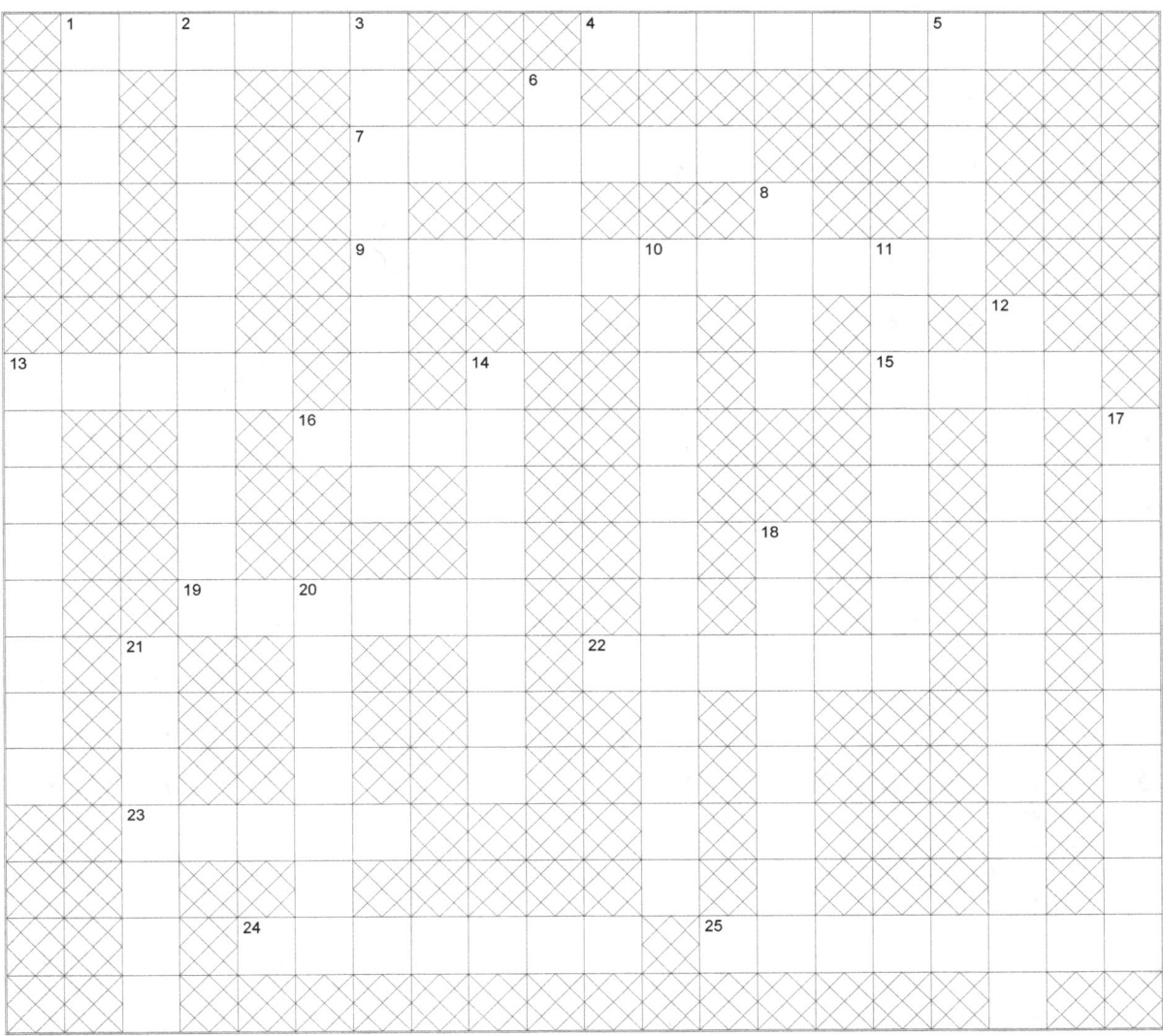

Across
1. Evoking feelings of repulsion
4. One of may kinds
7. Wished for longingly
9. Unnoticed
13. Age; time
15. In the middle of
16. Withered; dry
19. Exit; escape
22. Pale; dull
23. Bruised
24. Obstructed
25. Cloudy, misty, or hazy

Down
1. Eyes
2. Can't be turned back
3. Gave in
5. Easily understood; sane or rational
6. To bring distress or suffering to; plague
8. Manner
10. Faces
11. Inspired; captivated
12. Concealing one's true feelings or intentions
13. Euphoric; blissful
14. Scoffing; ridicule
17. Sensualness; voluptuousness
18. Responsible; at fault
20. A hymn, composition, or service for the dead
21. Majestic; inspiring awe; impressive

Poe Stories Vocabulary Crossword 4 Answer Key

Across
1. Evoking feelings of repulsion
4. One of may kinds
7. Wished for longingly
9. Unnoticed
13. Age; time
15. In the middle of
16. Withered; dry
19. Exit; escape
22. Pale; dull
23. Bruised
24. Obstructed
25. Cloudy, misty, or hazy

Down
1. Eyes
2. Can't be turned back
3. Gave in
5. Easily understood; sane or rational
6. To bring distress or suffering to; plague
8. Manner
10. Faces
11. Inspired; captivated
12. Concealing one's true feelings or intentions
13. Euphoric; blissful
14. Scoffing; ridicule
17. Sensualness; voluptuousness
18. Responsible; at fault
20. A hymn, composition, or service for the dead
21. Majestic; inspiring awe; impressive

Poe Stories Vocabulary Juggle Letters 1

1. DXVEE = 1. _____
   To bring distress or suffering to; plague

2. EEIURMQ = 2. _____
   A hymn, composition, or service for the dead

3. EUILSSSRNT = 3. _____
   Sensualness; voluptuousness

4. PMTYIUNI = 4. _____
   Exemption from punishment, penalty, or harm

5. OAUACGSSI = 5. _____
   Wise

6. ORSRCEOOTRBA = 6. _____
   To strengthen or support with other evidence

7. DAMI = 7. _____
   In the middle of

8. ANOEEVECMLL = 8. _____
   Ill will toward other; rancor; malice; evil influence, especially supernatural

9. IUDPSIOGRO = 9. _____
   Enormous

10. NIISDOER = 10. _____
    Scoffing; ridicule

11. DLIVI = 11. _____
    Bruised

12. UCLDI = 12. _____
    Easily understood; sane or rational

13. BRCOERELIVA = 13. _____
    Can't be turned back

14. ONUAEESNCCNT = 14. _____
    Faces

15. NEDCCIOEV = 15. _____
    To form or develop in the mind; devise

Poe Stories Vocabulary Juggle Letters 1 Answer Key

1. DXVEE = 1. VEXED
   To bring distress or suffering to; plague

2. EEIURMQ = 2. REQUIEM
   A hymn, composition, or service for the dead

3. EUILSSSRNT = 3. SULTRINESS
   Sensualness; voluptuousness

4. PMTYIUNI = 4. IMPUNITY
   Exemption from punishment, penalty, or harm

5. OAUACGSSI = 5. SAGACIOUS
   Wise

6. ORSRCEOOTRBA = 6. CORROBORATES
   To strengthen or support with other evidence

7. DAMI = 7. AMID
   In the middle of

8. ANOEEVECMLL = 8. MALEVOLENCE
   Ill will toward other; rancor; malice; evil influence, especially supernatural

9. IUDPSIOGRO = 9. PRODIGIOUS
   Enormous

10. NIISDOER = 10. DERISION
    Scoffing; ridicule

11. DLIVI = 11. LIVID
    Bruised

12. UCLDI = 12. LUCID
    Easily understood; sane or rational

13. BRCOERELIVA = 13. IRREVOCABLE
    Can't be turned back

14. ONUAEESNCCNT = 14. COUNTENANCES
    Faces

15. NEDCCIOEV = 15. CONCEIVED
    To form or develop in the mind; devise

Poe Stories Vocabulary Juggle Letters 2

1. TUEATS = 1. _____
   Shrewd

2. REES = 2. _____
   Withered; dry

3. NMEI = 3. _____
   Manner

4. CDBUESUMC = 4. _____
   Gave in

5. AITECTSC = 5. _____
   Euphoric; blissful

6. ESSLSIRTNU = 6. _____
   Sensualness; voluptuousness

7. MTUNIIPY = 7. _____
   Exemption from punishment, penalty, or harm

8. CVUPEEDNIER = 8. _____
   Unnoticed

9. MAID = 9. _____
   In the middle of

10. AILPDL = 10. _____
    Pale; dull

11. LEVCMONLEEA = 11. _____
    Ill will toward other; rancor; malice; evil influence, especially supernatural

12. DIIVL = 12. _____
    Bruised

13. SNRVEREPSSEE = 13. _____
    Quality of being directed away from what is right or good; an appalling action, situation or object

14. DFNMLAIO = 14. _____
    One of may kinds

15. HNITELNIAA = 15. _____
    To reduce to nonexistence; to nullify or render void; abolish

Poe Stories Vocabulary Juggle Letters 2 Answer Key

1. TUEATS = 1. ASTUTE
Shrewd

2. REES = 2. SERE
Withered; dry

3. NMEI = 3. MIEN
Manner

4. CDBUESUMC = 4. SUCCUMBED
Gave in

5. AITECTSC = 5. ECSTATIC
Euphoric; blissful

6. ESSLSIRTNU = 6. SULTRINESS
Sensualness; voluptuousness

7. MTUNIIPY = 7. IMPUNITY
Exemption from punishment, penalty, or harm

8. CVUPEEDNIER = 8. UNPERCEIVED
Unnoticed

9. MAID = 9. AMID
In the middle of

10. AILPDL = 10. PALLID
Pale; dull

11. LEVCMONLEEA = 11. MALEVOLENCE
Ill will toward other; rancor; malice; evil influence, especially supernatural

12. DIIVL = 12. LIVID
Bruised

13. SNRVEREPSSEE = 13. PERVERSENESS
Quality of being directed away from what is right or good; an appalling action, situation or object

14. DFNMLAIO = 14. MANIFOLD
One of may kinds

15. HNITELNIAA = 15. ANNIHILATE
To reduce to nonexistence; to nullify or render void; abolish

Poe Stories Vocabulary Juggle Letters 3

1. REPEESVSRNSE = 1. _____
Quality of being directed away from what is right or good; an appalling action, situation or object

2. EDIEMPD = 2. _____
Obstructed

3. EIONSDIR = 3. _____
Scoffing; ridicule

4. AERDMOEN = 4. _____
Inspired; captivated

5. PCLBLUAE = 5. _____
Responsible; at fault

6. OELVIBRAREC = 6. _____
Can't be turned back

7. DIPLAL = 7. _____
Pale; dull

8. IRSSLUSTEN = 8. _____
Sensualness; voluptuousness

9. NDUERSA = 9. _____
Into separate parts or pieces

10. RESESG =10. _____
Exit; escape

11. ROBS =11. _____
Eyes

12. DLIUC =12. _____
Easily understood; sane or rational

13. DVECOET =13. _____
Wished for longingly

14. ROROBAORCSTE =14. _____
To strengthen or support with other evidence

15. HOCPE =15. _____
Age; time

Poe Stories Vocabulary Juggle Letters 3 Answer Key

1. REPEESVSRNSE = 1. PERVERSENESS
   Quality of being directed away from what is right or good; an appalling action, situation or object

2. EDIEMPD = 2. IMPEDED
   Obstructed

3. EIONSDIR = 3. DERISION
   Scoffing; ridicule

4. AERDMOEN = 4. ENAMORED
   Inspired; captivated

5. PCLBLUAE = 5. CULPABLE
   Responsible; at fault

6. OELVIBRAREC = 6. IRREVOCABLE
   Can't be turned back

7. DIPLAL = 7. PALLID
   Pale; dull

8. IRSSLUSTEN = 8. SULTRINESS
   Sensualness; voluptuousness

9. NDUERSA = 9. ASUNDER
   Into separate parts or pieces

10. RESESG = 10. EGRESS
    Exit; escape

11. ROBS = 11. ORBS
    Eyes

12. DLIUC = 12. LUCID
    Easily understood; sane or rational

13. DVECOET = 13. COVETED
    Wished for longingly

14. ROROBAORCSTE = 14. CORROBORATES
    To strengthen or support with other evidence

15. HOCPE = 15. EPOCH
    Age; time

Poe Stories Vocabulary Juggle Letters 4

1. UNELOBUS = 1. _____
   Cloudy, misty, or hazy

2. IEMN = 2. _____
   Manner

3. NDREEOMA = 3. _____
   Inspired; captivated

4. IMUREQE = 4. _____
   A hymn, composition, or service for the dead

5. ACTISGYA = 5. _____
   The quality of being discerning, sound in judgement

6. NCVEPDIUREE = 6. _____
   Unnoticed

7. AEMEENLLOVC = 7. _____
   Ill will toward other; rancor; malice; evil influence, especially supernatural

8. IDAM = 8. _____
   In the middle of

9. IVONCEECD = 9. _____
   To form or develop in the mind; devise

10. TVDCOEE = 10. _____
    Wished for longingly

11. IGUNLIBEG = 11. _____
    Deceiving; diverting

12. TAIPPRINOA = 12. _____
    A ghostly figure

13. CASNRITAE = 13. _____
    To find out

14. BORELEIAVRC = 14. _____
    Can't be turned back

15. UITIPNYM = 15. _____
    Exemption from punishment, penalty, or harm

Poe Stories Vocabulary Juggle Letters 4

1. UNELOBUS = 1. NEBULOUS
   Cloudy, misty, or hazy

2. IEMN = 2. MIEN
   Manner

3. NDREEOMA = 3. ENAMORED
   Inspired; captivated

4. IMUREQE = 4. REQUIEM
   A hymn, composition, or service for the dead

5. ACTISGYA = 5. SAGACITY
   The quality of being discerning, sound in judgement

6. NCVEPDIUREE = 6. UNPERCEIVED
   Unnoticed

7. AEMEENLLOVC = 7. MALEVOLENCE
   Ill will toward other; rancor; malice; evil influence, especially supernatural

8. IDAM = 8. AMID
   In the middle of

9. IVONCEECD = 9. CONCEIVED
   To form or develop in the mind; devise

10. TVDCOEE =10. COVETED
    Wished for longingly

11. IGUNLIBEG =11. BEGUILING
    Deceiving; diverting

12. TAIPPRINOA =12. APPARITION
    A ghostly figure

13. CASNRITAE =13. ASCERTAIN
    To find out

14. BORELEIAVRC =14. IRREVOCABLE
    Can't be turned back

15. UITIPNYM =15. IMPUNITY
    Exemption from punishment, penalty, or harm

AMID	In the middle of
ANNIHILATE	To reduce to nonexistence; to nullify or render void; abolish
APPARITION	A ghostly figure
ASCERTAIN	To find out
ASTUTE	Shrewd

ASUNDER	Into separate parts or pieces
AUDACITY	Boldness; daring
BEGUILING	Deceiving; diverting
COGNIZANT	Aware; familiar with
CONCEIVED	To form or develop in the mind; devise

CONSIGNED	Handed over
CORROBORATES	To strengthen or support with other evidence
COUNTENANCES	Faces
COVETED	Wished for longingly
CULPABLE	Responsible; at fault

DERISION	Scoffing; ridicule
DISSIMULATION	Concealing one's true feelings or intentions
ECSTATIC	Euphoric; blissful
EGREGIOUS	Bad or offensive
EGRESS	Exit; escape

ENAMORED	Inspired; captivated
EPOCH	Age; time
IMPEDED	Obstructed
IMPUNITY	Exemption from punishment, penalty, or harm
IRREVOCABLE	Can't be turned back

LIVID	Bruised
LUCID	Easily understood; sane or rational
MALEVOLENCE	Ill will toward other; rancor; malice; evil influence, especially supernatural
MANIFOLD	One of may kinds
MIEN	Manner

NEBULOUS	Cloudy, misty, or hazy
ODIOUS	Evoking feelings of repulsion
ORBS	Eyes
PALLID	Pale; dull
PERVERSENESS	Quality of being directed away from what is right or good; an appalling action, situation or object

PRODIGIOUS	Enormous
PROMISCUOUSLY	Causally; randomly
REQUIEM	A hymn, composition, or service for the dead
SAGACIOUS	Wise
SAGACITY	The quality of being discerning, sound in judgement

SERE	Withered; dry
SUBLIME	Majestic; inspiring awe; impressive
SUCCUMBED	Gave in
SULTRINESS	Sensualness; voluptuousness
UNPERCEIVED	Unnoticed

VEXED	To bring distress or suffering to; plague
VORACITY	Wild hunger

Poe Stories Vocabulary

ASUNDER	BEGUILING	CULPABLE	PALLID	COUNTENANCES
IMPUNITY	NEBULOUS	ORBS	ODIOUS	COGNIZANT
CORROBORATES	ASTUTE	FREE SPACE	IMPEDED	EGREGIOUS
LIVID	SUCCUMBED	EPOCH	DISSIMULATION	APPARITION
AMID	VEXED	MIEN	VORACITY	SAGACIOUS

Poe Stories Vocabulary

PERVERSENESS	SAGACITY	PROMISCUOUSLY	EGRESS	COVETED
SUBLIME	PRODIGIOUS	MANIFOLD	CONSIGNED	LUCID
REQUIEM	ANNIHILATE	FREE SPACE	MALEVOLENCE	SERE
SULTRINESS	DERISION	ECSTATIC	ENAMORED	UNPERCEIVED
ASCERTAIN	AUDACITY	SAGACIOUS	VORACITY	MIEN

Poe Stories Vocabulary

EGREGIOUS	SULTRINESS	SAGACITY	AUDACITY	AMID
EPOCH	MANIFOLD	NEBULOUS	CORROBORATES	CONSIGNED
COGNIZANT	ASTUTE	FREE SPACE	CULPABLE	ORBS
SAGACIOUS	PRODIGIOUS	LUCID	ODIOUS	PERVERSENESS
DISSIMULATION	DERISION	PROMISCUOUSLY	EGRESS	REQUIEM

Poe Stories Vocabulary

PALLID	ECSTATIC	ANNIHILATE	SERE	MIEN
ASCERTAIN	SUBLIME	COUNTENANCES	APPARITION	MALEVOLENCE
VORACITY	IMPUNITY	FREE SPACE	BEGUILING	ENAMORED
VEXED	CONCEIVED	UNPERCEIVED	ASUNDER	SUCCUMBED
IMPEDED	COVETED	REQUIEM	EGRESS	PROMISCUOUSLY

Poe Stories Vocabulary

COUNTENANCES	CULPABLE	VORACITY	ASUNDER	SERE
PERVERSENESS	DERISION	VEXED	PRODIGIOUS	LUCID
SULTRINESS	ENAMORED	FREE SPACE	PROMISCUOUSLY	MANIFOLD
SAGACITY	IMPEDED	MIEN	IMPUNITY	SAGACIOUS
SUCCUMBED	MALEVOLENCE	IRREVOCABLE	COGNIZANT	REQUIEM

Poe Stories Vocabulary

COVETED	UNPERCEIVED	NEBULOUS	LIVID	AUDACITY
CONCEIVED	ECSTATIC	ANNIHILATE	CORROBORATES	ASCERTAIN
ODIOUS	BEGUILING	FREE SPACE	CONSIGNED	EPOCH
SUBLIME	APPARITION	ASTUTE	AMID	PALLID
ORBS	DISSIMULATION	REQUIEM	COGNIZANT	IRREVOCABLE

Poe Stories Vocabulary

MALEVOLENCE	IMPEDED	DISSIMULATION	CONSIGNED	COGNIZANT
EGRESS	ODIOUS	IMPUNITY	NEBULOUS	SUCCUMBED
COVETED	COUNTENANCES	FREE SPACE	PROMISCUOUSLY	CORROBORATES
DERISION	PALLID	SERE	ECSTATIC	BEGUILING
EPOCH	ASUNDER	IRREVOCABLE	VEXED	ORBS

Poe Stories Vocabulary

SAGACIOUS	AUDACITY	VORACITY	AMID	LIVID
MIEN	UNPERCEIVED	ASTUTE	SUBLIME	CONCEIVED
CULPABLE	REQUIEM	FREE SPACE	EGREGIOUS	LUCID
APPARITION	ASCERTAIN	ENAMORED	SAGACITY	PERVERSENESS
ANNIHILATE	PRODIGIOUS	ORBS	VEXED	IRREVOCABLE

Poe Stories Vocabulary

DISSIMULATION	EPOCH	LIVID	ASUNDER	AMID
NEBULOUS	SERE	AUDACITY	SUBLIME	IRREVOCABLE
CULPABLE	ECSTATIC	FREE SPACE	UNPERCEIVED	PERVERSENESS
CONSIGNED	ASCERTAIN	ENAMORED	SAGACITY	PROMISCUOUSLY
IMPEDED	PRODIGIOUS	EGRESS	SAGACIOUS	MIEN

Poe Stories Vocabulary

VEXED	IMPUNITY	MANIFOLD	SULTRINESS	COGNIZANT
VORACITY	COVETED	MALEVOLENCE	APPARITION	DERISION
ODIOUS	BEGUILING	FREE SPACE	SUCCUMBED	PALLID
ANNIHILATE	ASTUTE	EGREGIOUS	LUCID	REQUIEM
CORROBORATES	COUNTENANCES	MIEN	SAGACIOUS	EGRESS

Poe Stories Vocabulary

NEBULOUS	ASUNDER	UNPERCEIVED	PERVERSENESS	LUCID
PRODIGIOUS	AUDACITY	SAGACIOUS	IRREVOCABLE	VORACITY
PROMISCUOUSLY	CONCEIVED	FREE SPACE	SUBLIME	SUCCUMBED
REQUIEM	SERE	CONSIGNED	SULTRINESS	MIEN
VEXED	MALEVOLENCE	IMPEDED	ANNIHILATE	ASTUTE

Poe Stories Vocabulary

ENAMORED	EGREGIOUS	APPARITION	IMPUNITY	ORBS
DERISION	EGRESS	COUNTENANCES	DISSIMULATION	AMID
BEGUILING	CORROBORATES	FREE SPACE	ODIOUS	MANIFOLD
ASCERTAIN	COVETED	SAGACITY	ECSTATIC	EPOCH
PALLID	CULPABLE	ASTUTE	ANNIHILATE	IMPEDED

Poe Stories Vocabulary

NEBULOUS	PRODIGIOUS	LUCID	PROMISCUOUSLY	CONCEIVED
ECSTATIC	MANIFOLD	IMPEDED	IRREVOCABLE	PALLID
EGREGIOUS	ANNIHILATE	FREE SPACE	COVETED	SUCCUMBED
CULPABLE	SAGACITY	DISSIMULATION	VORACITY	ASCERTAIN
VEXED	COUNTENANCES	LIVID	ASTUTE	COGNIZANT

Poe Stories Vocabulary

PERVERSENESS	SAGACIOUS	AUDACITY	CORROBORATES	IMPUNITY
CONSIGNED	UNPERCEIVED	AMID	EGRESS	REQUIEM
SUBLIME	EPOCH	FREE SPACE	SULTRINESS	SERE
ODIOUS	BEGUILING	ENAMORED	MALEVOLENCE	ASUNDER
MIEN	ORBS	COGNIZANT	ASTUTE	LIVID

Poe Stories Vocabulary

ANNIHILATE	NEBULOUS	VEXED	ODIOUS	ECSTATIC
AMID	DERISION	LIVID	SULTRINESS	SAGACIOUS
PROMISCUOUSLY	MALEVOLENCE	FREE SPACE	REQUIEM	SUBLIME
MANIFOLD	IMPUNITY	SUCCUMBED	ORBS	APPARITION
AUDACITY	COUNTENANCES	ASCERTAIN	EPOCH	SERE

Poe Stories Vocabulary

PERVERSENESS	EGRESS	IRREVOCABLE	PRODIGIOUS	ASTUTE
ENAMORED	PALLID	COVETED	BEGUILING	CONCEIVED
LUCID	MIEN	FREE SPACE	CORROBORATES	CONSIGNED
DISSIMULATION	EGREGIOUS	ASUNDER	CULPABLE	VORACITY
UNPERCEIVED	COGNIZANT	SERE	EPOCH	ASCERTAIN

Poe Stories Vocabulary

VORACITY	SAGACITY	ASTUTE	PALLID	PRODIGIOUS
SUCCUMBED	MANIFOLD	ASUNDER	CONSIGNED	AUDACITY
LUCID	SUBLIME	FREE SPACE	ODIOUS	AMID
IMPUNITY	SAGACIOUS	DISSIMULATION	IRREVOCABLE	CULPABLE
UNPERCEIVED	DERISION	CONCEIVED	MALEVOLENCE	IMPEDED

Poe Stories Vocabulary

ASCERTAIN	CORROBORATES	LIVID	ANNIHILATE	EPOCH
ECSTATIC	SULTRINESS	VEXED	EGRESS	ENAMORED
REQUIEM	COUNTENANCES	FREE SPACE	COVETED	PROMISCUOUSLY
COGNIZANT	BEGUILING	PERVERSENESS	APPARITION	ORBS
SERE	EGREGIOUS	IMPEDED	MALEVOLENCE	CONCEIVED

Poe Stories Vocabulary

VORACITY	PROMISCUOUSLY	EPOCH	IRREVOCABLE	LUCID
SERE	ENAMORED	ASUNDER	SAGACITY	CONCEIVED
REQUIEM	CONSIGNED	FREE SPACE	SULTRINESS	IMPEDED
ORBS	COUNTENANCES	ODIOUS	COVETED	PRODIGIOUS
PALLID	EGREGIOUS	EGRESS	ASTUTE	SUCCUMBED

Poe Stories Vocabulary

AUDACITY	COGNIZANT	CORROBORATES	CULPABLE	AMID
APPARITION	ASCERTAIN	ECSTATIC	MIEN	DISSIMULATION
DERISION	PERVERSENESS	FREE SPACE	BEGUILING	SAGACIOUS
VEXED	MALEVOLENCE	UNPERCEIVED	ANNIHILATE	NEBULOUS
IMPUNITY	SUBLIME	SUCCUMBED	ASTUTE	EGRESS

Poe Stories Vocabulary

LIVID	MIEN	AUDACITY	PERVERSENESS	LUCID
EGRESS	IMPUNITY	VORACITY	REQUIEM	NEBULOUS
APPARITION	CONCEIVED	FREE SPACE	COGNIZANT	DISSIMULATION
IRREVOCABLE	ASCERTAIN	SAGACIOUS	ECSTATIC	CONSIGNED
EGREGIOUS	SULTRINESS	ASTUTE	MALEVOLENCE	PROMISCUOUSLY

Poe Stories Vocabulary

UNPERCEIVED	SERE	CULPABLE	COVETED	AMID
ODIOUS	BEGUILING	SUBLIME	MANIFOLD	PALLID
SAGACITY	PRODIGIOUS	FREE SPACE	ENAMORED	COUNTENANCES
ANNIHILATE	CORROBORATES	SUCCUMBED	ASUNDER	ORBS
IMPEDED	VEXED	PROMISCUOUSLY	MALEVOLENCE	ASTUTE

Poe Stories Vocabulary

IRREVOCABLE	DERISION	ASTUTE	NEBULOUS	BEGUILING
APPARITION	SUCCUMBED	ANNIHILATE	LIVID	ASUNDER
CORROBORATES	MIEN	FREE SPACE	EPOCH	PRODIGIOUS
IMPUNITY	REQUIEM	LUCID	ECSTATIC	ENAMORED
ODIOUS	SULTRINESS	ORBS	PROMISCUOUSLY	VEXED

Poe Stories Vocabulary

EGREGIOUS	CONCEIVED	COGNIZANT	MALEVOLENCE	SUBLIME
CONSIGNED	SAGACITY	PALLID	SAGACIOUS	UNPERCEIVED
COUNTENANCES	SERE	FREE SPACE	PERVERSENESS	CULPABLE
EGRESS	AMID	ASCERTAIN	AUDACITY	VORACITY
DISSIMULATION	IMPEDED	VEXED	PROMISCUOUSLY	ORBS

Poe Stories Vocabulary

ECSTATIC	MANIFOLD	ODIOUS	PERVERSENESS	VORACITY
ASUNDER	ORBS	REQUIEM	APPARITION	LUCID
PROMISCUOUSLY	NEBULOUS	FREE SPACE	CONCEIVED	COVETED
AMID	PRODIGIOUS	IRREVOCABLE	SERE	AUDACITY
COUNTENANCES	SUBLIME	SUCCUMBED	VEXED	DERISION

Poe Stories Vocabulary

EGREGIOUS	ASTUTE	CULPABLE	SAGACIOUS	COGNIZANT
MALEVOLENCE	MIEN	EGRESS	ANNIHILATE	UNPERCEIVED
LIVID	SULTRINESS	FREE SPACE	ASCERTAIN	SAGACITY
IMPUNITY	PALLID	ENAMORED	EPOCH	CORROBORATES
IMPEDED	DISSIMULATION	DERISION	VEXED	SUCCUMBED

Poe Stories Vocabulary

ENAMORED	NEBULOUS	CONCEIVED	ANNIHILATE	AMID
ASTUTE	REQUIEM	CORROBORATES	IMPEDED	AUDACITY
LUCID	SERE	FREE SPACE	SAGACITY	EPOCH
ASCERTAIN	MIEN	VORACITY	BEGUILING	CONSIGNED
SULTRINESS	PALLID	ORBS	IRREVOCABLE	COVETED

Poe Stories Vocabulary

IMPUNITY	MALEVOLENCE	VEXED	EGRESS	PERVERSENESS
PRODIGIOUS	DISSIMULATION	MANIFOLD	CULPABLE	APPARITION
DERISION	SUBLIME	FREE SPACE	LIVID	EGREGIOUS
UNPERCEIVED	COGNIZANT	SUCCUMBED	ODIOUS	COUNTENANCES
PROMISCUOUSLY	SAGACIOUS	COVETED	IRREVOCABLE	ORBS

Poe Stories Vocabulary

APPARITION	DERISION	CORROBORATES	EGRESS	SERE
AUDACITY	LUCID	CONSIGNED	COGNIZANT	ANNIHILATE
IMPUNITY	ASUNDER	FREE SPACE	CONCEIVED	VEXED
ORBS	CULPABLE	ASCERTAIN	PROMISCUOUSLY	UNPERCEIVED
PRODIGIOUS	ASTUTE	SAGACITY	MALEVOLENCE	SAGACIOUS

Poe Stories Vocabulary

SUBLIME	IMPEDED	IRREVOCABLE	ODIOUS	EGREGIOUS
MIEN	REQUIEM	DISSIMULATION	ENAMORED	ECSTATIC
COUNTENANCES	MANIFOLD	FREE SPACE	PALLID	VORACITY
EPOCH	SUCCUMBED	AMID	COVETED	NEBULOUS
SULTRINESS	PERVERSENESS	SAGACIOUS	MALEVOLENCE	SAGACITY

Poe Stories Vocabulary

MANIFOLD	CONCEIVED	DISSIMULATION	REQUIEM	ENAMORED
ORBS	COUNTENANCES	ASTUTE	NEBULOUS	IMPUNITY
SERE	PERVERSENESS	FREE SPACE	PROMISCUOUSLY	COVETED
SAGACITY	EGRESS	ASUNDER	LUCID	SUCCUMBED
ANNIHILATE	VORACITY	PRODIGIOUS	APPARITION	IRREVOCABLE

Poe Stories Vocabulary

ASCERTAIN	AMID	EPOCH	SUBLIME	COGNIZANT
PALLID	ODIOUS	UNPERCEIVED	BEGUILING	CONSIGNED
MIEN	SAGACIOUS	FREE SPACE	AUDACITY	CORROBORATES
LIVID	VEXED	EGREGIOUS	IMPEDED	CULPABLE
DERISION	SULTRINESS	IRREVOCABLE	APPARITION	PRODIGIOUS

www.ingramcontent.com/pod-product-compliance
Lightning Source LLC
Chambersburg PA
CBHW081454070526
44586CB00019B/2348